ZERO
PERCENT CHANCE

A Tribute to the Heroes of Cross-Functional
Team Manbij: A Soldier's Memoir

MAJOR JON AND SAMANTHA TURNBULL

WESTBOW
PRESS®
A DIVISION OF THOMAS NELSON
& ZONDERVAN

This book is a work of non-fiction. Unless otherwise noted, the author and the publisher make no explicit guarantees as to the accuracy of the information contained in this book and in some cases, names of people and places have been altered to protect their privacy.

WestBow Press books may be ordered through booksellers or by contacting:

WestBow Press
A Division of Thomas Nelson & Zondervan
1663 Liberty Drive
Bloomington, IN 47403
www.westbowpress.com
844-714-3454

Because of the dynamic nature of the Internet, any web addresses or links contained in this book may have changed since publication and may no longer be valid. The views expressed in this work are solely those of the author and do not necessarily reflect the views of the publisher, and the publisher hereby disclaims any responsibility for them.

Any people depicted in stock imagery provided by Getty Images are models, and such images are being used for illustrative purposes only. Certain stock imagery © Getty Images.

Scriptures taken from the Holy Bible, New International Version®, NIV®. Copyright © 1973, 1978, 1984, 2011 by Biblica, Inc.™ Used by permission of Zondervan. All rights reserved worldwide. www.zondervan.com The "NIV" and "New International Version" are trademarks registered in the United States Patent and Trademark Office by Biblica, Inc.®

ISBN: 978-1-6642-4328-6 (sc)
ISBN: 978-1-6642-4329-3 (hc)
ISBN: 978-1-6642-4330-9 (e)

Library of Congress Control Number: 2021917216

Print information available on the last page.

WestBow Press rev. date: 9/13/2021

Dedicated to all gold star family members: you are loved. A grateful nation thanks you for your sacrifice to provide the blanket of freedom under which we reside.

To those heroes who made sure I lived and make sure I continue to live: Devin, Joe, Twerp, Dr. Kyle, Neil, Roland, medics in Syria, medics in Iraq, medics and hospital nurses at LRMC, and medics and nurses at WRNMMC and 4 Center. Above all else, members of the Care Coalition, Heidi and Justin, and my amazing strength and conditioning coaches at the THOR3 gym at Fort Bragg: we owe you everything!

My family: Samantha, Ian, Dad, Mom, Lizard-breath, my in-laws, my many aunts and uncles, Mo, Rania, my precious goddaughter Rain, Sophie, Tabitha, Devin, Betsy, Pricilla, Preston, Amina ("Little Mama"), Dave, Mama Fran, and Mama Sandy and Jack. Also, those who ensured I was cared for in Syria: Dr. Reem, Mona, and Furat Hospital nurses and doctors. To everyone who came to visit me on the long days I spent in hospitals, and for those of you who believed in me when I was at my worst.

Finally, my recovery would not have been possible without the mention of many inspiring individuals who took the time out of their busy schedules to stop by my hospital room and spread a little cheer. Chaplain Braswell, you prayed over me every day. After our long talks about Hadassah and the possibility of Sam and me adopting, you prayed that God would give us a child, either naturally or through adoption. Because of that prayer, I am happy to tell you, Samantha and I welcomed our little miracle on February 2, 2021, the day before Ghadir's birthday. In honor of Team Manbij, we named our son Scotty Jon. And he has the best nickname, "Little Twerp," after my hero.

Finally, my teammates and brothers: 1/1, 2/1, Team Manbij, Ninety-Sixth Civil Affairs Battalion (minus) soldiers, Category 613, and my Red Platoon soldiers in Apache Troop.

A special mention to the prayer warriors out there. God heard your prayers and protected me. Thanks to Saint John's Catholic Church, the Nazarene Church, missionaries in India, the many churches around the States, and everyone who saw my need and lifted their voices to God, especially our friends and family who prayed for me at seven in the morning and seven in the evening! We love you all!

Marching Orders: I, Jonathan Turnbull, now Major Turnbull, US Army, issue this order to all Americans who, in reading this, want to help our heroes: My friend NLT Close of Business (COB) today reaches out to that soldier or veteran in order to give him or her an ear to talk over the worst days of his or her life and start healing, knowing that he or she is loved. On order, I offer this advice/command: "You are stronger than this, and you can overcome it. We got this! In everything, remember, Victory Above Loss."

If you want to donate to a just and honorable cause, I recommend the following organizations, which have resources available to heal the United States' wounded warriors and gold star families: We Got This Foundation (www.wegotthis.org) was set up by my January 16 sister Tabitha to help our gold star children in the wake of the terrorist attack of January 16, 2019. The Veteran Airlift Command, a nonprofit, provides air travel to our veterans at no cost to the veteran. Other organizations include the Wounded Warrior Program, the Semper Fi Fund, the Robert Irvine Foundation, and any USO.

This document does not contain any classified or secret information to the best of my knowledge.
//original signed Jonathan Turnbull//

To the best of my knowledge this document does not contain any classified information.

Jonathan M Turnbull

Captain, US Army

INTRODUCTION

How does one write an account that honors one's fallen teammates when every word in every line sends sharp stinging arrows of pain straight to the heart? As the team commander, I choose to undertake this feat, even relishing the pain that I know it will bring. I know the caliber of the individuals whom God gave me the honor of not only serving alongside but also loving in a way that only servicemembers who have served overseas in combat truly understand. For that I apologize in advance, because I am neither a well-spoken individual nor an English major. This is going to be a lot of rough storytelling at its finest, meant to be heard around a campfire or at the bar in a VFW.

I am Captain Jonathan Turnbull of the US Army. This story is about my time fighting ISIS in Syria. It is also a tribute to the other members of my team, Cross-Functional Team Manbij, which consisted of multiple Special Forces soldiers, numerous special operations soldiers, two naval sailors, and the most wonderful linguist. This story demonstrates how the US military can fight an enemy through unconventional means. My team undermined ISIS by enhancing the legitimacy of the local government. We enabled the local government to have girls return to school after seven years away. We helped turn the power on for northeast Syria while empowering the local medical system. Our success in these areas made us the target of an ISIS suicide bomber. The explosion killed four American heroes, wounded three Americans, and injured and killed many local Syrian nationals.

I remember my youth pastor Gary telling me after I had run headfirst into a tree while playing baseball, scraping my face and nose up, that I needed to turn my frown upside down. It was wintertime. I had a bright red scab on my nose. It was Christmastime, and there was a famous reindeer that Santa used to pull his sled because the reindeer had a bright red nose. That brightened my day then, and the phrase "Turn your frown upside down," along with the life lesson, stuck with me. After I'd heard that, I would attempt to find happiness in every situation, thus cultivating humor as my coping mechanism for whatever should come.

While lying in my hospital bed for long hours—and by long hours, I mean all day, every day, all week long—I had a hard time finding joy in anything. I went from being one of the most important individuals in the region, working out at least three times a day and with a beautiful head of hair and a nice full beard, to being a shell of a man who couldn't see, who had no hair on his head, who had no beard / face armor, who was void of clothing (nothing new there), and who felt alone. After being told what had happened, I listened to the video of the attack on YouTube and multiple news stations. I found myself with no purpose. I was trying to figure out how to convince my nurses or any passerby to unplug my machines so I could join my soldiers and lead them into the last great fight. Yes, I was suicidal. As I write this two years later, I choke back the tears in remembrance of those I love, thinking that they had to make the journey without me. I know that they were okay because they were each escorted by God into heaven, but I would have wanted to be there with them, standing strong, shoulder to shoulder, as their brother, accountable to answering for whatever.

I know that I cannot negotiate with God for the acceptance of my brothers and sisters, but I wanted to be there to see the archangel Michael, commander of the angel armies, throw his temper tantrum when my chief was appointed the new commander. I would have been the loudest clapper and my chief's guidon-bearer as long as the archangel Michael allowed me to break his ranks. So, while I was lying there asking God for death, a thought popped into my head: My military team family was in heaven and were grateful to be at the roundtable eating my great-grandma's cinnamon rolls, but I could still be with my family here on earth. And I needed to be thankful for this opportunity how?

I know that I am rambling. As I pour my heart and soul into this, there is something you are trying to decipher, my dear reader. This is my disclaimer: Every person mentioned herein, along with any dates, locations, and events, is based on someone or something real; however, any exaggerations are an error on the author's part. Some names have been changed, shortened, or used as nicknames. I've done this for privacy, at the request of the individuals involved.

I hope that you can forgive me, knowing that I suffered severe trauma to my brain and was unconscious for much of my recovery. The following is from accounts that have been told to my wife and me: Following the explosion, I had twenty-two lifesaving surgeries in Syria, Iraq, Germany, and the USA. Samantha, my wife and coauthor, was kept informed at each leg of my journey home. Additionally, she has helped me write *Zero Percent Chance* on our computer, acting as my proofreader and editor, which was an incredible task since I cannot see and it is rather difficult for me to use a computer. Thankfully she kept a journal throughout our journey to help make this a bit easier. I tell the story from my standpoint, but everything is verified by my wife and the other survivors of the suicide bombing in Manbij, Syria, on January 16, 2019.

I write this account for my family, which includes not only my blood but also my January 16 military team family. There is a special bond between soldiers on a deployment that is very difficult to explain. The HBO television series *Band of Brothers* serves as a very accurate representation of this relationship.

Back to my sad story: Lying in my hospital bed, I needed a purpose. I decided I needed help to heal not only my war wounds but also the emotional injuries from having my loved ones ripped away from my soul—the injuries that the doctors couldn't heal. I took on the emotional trauma of my loved ones' family members, which had to be far greater than any of my paper cuts. I was a funny guy, which I knew because every time someone came into my room, they laughed—hopefully with me and not at me.

I needed a mission. *Jon, your mission, should you choose to accept it, is to cheer up your new family. Bring joy, dry their tears, and make sure everyone is always happy.* The mission sounded good in my head. Eating a hospital omelet with toast and coffee in the morning, I had a smile on my face (probably because my wife was on her way with my second breakfast) and knew that there was a faint glow surrounding me. I was wrapped in my heated blanket, so I was warm, ready to start not only my day but also my new life.

Very often I sit alone in the dark that surrounds me and I wonder if what I did was worth it and if my family and friends have suffered in vain. I have learned that life is precious and that some lives are far more important than others.

As far as freedom goes, our small surgical strike team was the tip of the spear. I heard a high-ranking military official congratulate my wife, saying that it was Team Manbij that had led President Trump to make the call to begin the assault that removed ISIS from Syria and Iraq. We mapped out the ISIS network in our area of operations, ensuring the elimination of fifteen hundred ISIS fighters from our area, and through our operations we made sure they did not have a leg to stand on while we legitimized the local government in the eyes of the population and delegitimized any minor faction of ISIS.

On January 17, eighty-eight thousand ISIS members were eliminated. This was accomplished by changing the rate of flow of the Euphrates River and working with the hydroelectric dam, along with enhancing the capability of the education system to facilitate the increase in the number of students. Most of our actions were done through diplomatic channels. Echoing President Teddy Roosevelt's "Speak softly ..." motto, we were the big stick at times, ensuring that security and lethality was always first while planning not to give any malevolent actors a foothold in the area. We proved that it was possible to execute the orders of Chaos 1 before he resigned from office and, as General Mattis said, to "smile, but always have a plan to murder everyone in the room."

We acted with kindness in every operation, showing the people in northeast Syria that coalition forces were not a conquering force but a partner in the area. We were there to provide help, with the intent to get the northeastern Syrians back on their feet at any cost, which we did. We showed the world that while we acted with what seemed like kindness, we were able not only to alleviate suffering but also to accomplish our military end of denying ISIS the ability to terrorize the local population and continue to strengthen their hold in the Middle East.

So, to answer my initial question, yes, what we did was worth it. To my friends and family, I pray that you will forgive me, as I will one day forgive myself. But I am proud of my scars and will always wear them as a badge of honor, telling the world about the four heroes of Manbij who saved the world. My friends, my family, my loved ones: until we meet again.

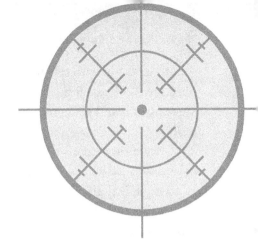

1

Let's Do This

Commit your work to the Lord, and your plans will be established.

—Proverbs 16:3

I have always been a man of action. My mother and father knew this. It was for this reason that they pulled me out of school in the fifth grade, when my grades began suffering. Their reasoning was that I would learn far better doing, rather than just reading and being told. In my years of education that followed, I learned quickly through action and relished the opportunity to attempt new things because I knew that I needed just one try and I would be capable of unlimited possibilities. I learned through trial and error. ADHD was not a thing when I was a child, but if it were, I would have been tied up and had medicine poured down my throat because I was always active.

Nothing changed once I joined the army. I attended West Point, became an officer, and progressed along until I became a captain at Fort Bragg. I found myself living the perfect life. I had the perfect wife who complemented me in every way. Samantha was everything that I was not. She was beautiful, kind, caring, compassionate, and smart—and super weird, because for some unknown reason she liked me. We had a little boy; his name was Ian, and he is the most amazing human being on the face of the planet. I couldn't wait to train him to be a man and have him as a best friend.

I had a great career. I was a team leader in special operations. Everyone called it a Special Forces team, but we were so much more. We were a civil affairs team that focused on getting people to do what we wanted them to do, without force if possible. My team was capable of negotiation, and I saw them do things that impressed me beyond words. We could gain unlimited access and influence in areas that were completely closed off to nonlocal populations. Even though we were the best who walked around our area, I always looked for an opportunity to shine. Continuing to network even at Fort Bragg, for practice of course, I found myself sitting in a video teleconference explaining how a civil affairs planning team would benefit any organization because we would be able to provide in-depth, relevant planning capabilities regarding effects on the local populations and the second- and third-order effects of operations on the population with regard to unconventional warfare (UW). This was not nearly as intelligent as my executive officer's elevator pitch, which I needed to memorize, because after my boss Major Nick had finished talking, he asked for our team to join his organization on a quick deployment to the Middle East. If we were to augment the unit we were briefing on the video teleconference, then we could help increase the effectiveness of Nick's deployment through cross-unit communication. The objective would be to fight against the terrorist organization known as the Islamic State. Each of us around the table threw a thumbs-up, signaling that we would make it happen with further coordination. Then the planning began.

My five-man team occupied the conference room for the next four weeks, filling up each of the whiteboards with writing regarding the Military Decision-Making Process (MDMP). We packed up our equipment and made sure our paperwork, wills, and any legal documents were in order before meeting at the compound on

September 1, 2018. Prior to the meet-up, I kissed my beautiful wife goodbye, knowing for some reason this was likely the last time I would ever see her again. I hugged my son and said a quick prayer before grabbing my best friend and right-hand man, Chief Michael. Chief Michael and I had worked together in our battalion for the last four years as a civil affairs planning team. When planning this deployment, Michael was the first guy whom I knew I wanted going with me to Iraq. His sense of humor, can-do attitude, and positivity were crucial while I was away from my family. Being the "old broken man" he is from serving ten-plus years prior as an army airborne soldier, Michael was now on his last deployment, one we were both very eager for and enthusiastic about. We turned to enter the compound to begin our deployment.

As weird as it may sound, a deployment is what we live for in the army. I joined the army not only to serve my country but also to serve through deploying. It was through deploying that I felt alive, because on deployments I was able to keep the monsters away from my loved ones, preserving freedom and keeping the country that I love so much free from terrorism and oppression. The only problem with deployments is that after a deployment, no matter what happens or fails to happen, most soldiers do not return in the same condition in which they left.

My family and the families of millions of soldiers past, present, and future know that soldiers change with the high tempo of deploying, especially in special operations. For example, while working at Fort Stewart, Georgia, ten days after my son was born, I deployed for nine months to Afghanistan. This was in September of 2012. I came home, and a month later, in July 2013, I applied and volunteered for the civil affairs selection course at Fort Bragg, North Carolina. One of a handful of soldiers selected for this special operations unit, I started schooling and training for eighteen months. As soon as I graduated in September 2015, I left for a six-month deployment to Jordan. I was home for four months, then went to Lebanon, and three months later went to Jordan for another six months. Each time I returned, Samantha had to learn who the man who had returned was. Sadly, of the last five years, I was gone for four, and Samantha felt that it was like having a stranger come home and live with her. Reintegration became ever more important after each deployment. It allowed me to get to know how I had changed and to help my family understand who I was. I leaned heavily on my teammates, such as Chief Michael, during the return, which is why I ended up seriously attaching myself to him for this deployment.

So, back to September 1, 2018. Michael and I waved goodbye to our families as we entered the compound. Then we and the other soldiers boarded the buses to take us to the flight line. It hurts knowing how much harder deployments are for spouses. Our spouses need to drive home with emotions that are indescribable. They drive away having to hide their fear and tears from our children, who don't fully understand what is going on. Then they return to their homes alone, not knowing when or if we will return, to take on the task of being both parents. And eventually they must go to sleep in beds that feel very cold and lonely. It's no surprise when we find out that they end up sleeping with the children to fill the void of loneliness. Schooling, homework, sports, bills, and family drama all continue, and they get to do it with grace. On top of all that, the dreaded "Deployment Murphy" moves in with them. From what my wife tells me, Murphy is the worst roommate in the world. Murphy's luggage includes every adult nightmare possible. Instantly a perfect home will have severe plumbing issues, or a brand-new car will have troubles that aren't normally present. Though this sounds normal, it isn't. For instance, two days after I left with Chief Michael, Hurricane Dorian (category 5) made landfall on North Carolina. Once it had passed, two weeks later another hit. Roads washed out and flooding was everywhere, leaving everyone stuck at home for weeks, some without power. Murphy's Law says that anything that can go wrong will go wrong, so the nickname Deployment Murphy is quite fitting. Yet through it all, our spouses do what they need to do, sometimes leaning on other military spouses to get through everything, unfortunately living every day in fear, wondering if soldiers will come knock on their door.

Such is not the case for us soldiers. We are together, joking around and preparing for a grand adventure, with an air of excitement surrounding us. I know without a doubt that military spouses have one of the hardest jobs in the world and are a force to be reckoned with.

The day we were leaving for Iraq was unique. The C-17 airplane that would take us across the pond was not working. After our bags were weighed, we were put on standby and then told to return tomorrow at the same time. We all laughed and called our families to ask them to return. Once they had done so, we met them in the parking lot. After our reunion embraces, we returned home without notifying our unit so they couldn't tell us to come into work. As I had told my guys, "Yeah, that isn't going to happen."

This routine of showing up, saying our goodbyes, wiping away tears, calling our families back, and then ignoring or even blatantly avoiding work to spend time with my family because the air force couldn't repair the door on the plane occurred for the next four days. Though this week ended up being extremely emotionally exhausting, I will forever be grateful for it and the extra time to spend with Sam and Ian. On September 6, I and the other guys in my unit finally found ourselves on the bird and taxiing on the runway, preparing to take off. As the bird prepared to take off, Chief and I made sure to prepare the most essential comfort item for the journey: our hammocks.

During the week while the bird was "broken," I was shopping at Walmart with my wife. While walking down the camping aisle, I saw the two-person (couples') hammocks and took a quick picture with my phone. Joking around like I always do, I sent the picture to Chief, asking if he wanted me to get the hammock so we could cuddle on the plane. He responded instantly with a picture of a single-person hammock at the Walmart he was shopping at with his wife at the same moment and said he was getting a single-person one for us. That was when I knew he and I were going to be kindred spirits during the deployment.

I made sure Chief knew that I had allowed him the prime real estate for his hammock on the outside. We had our sleeping setups completed before the plane was in the air, and we were finished early enough to help the air force airmen with their hammocks. The airmen would be sleeping by our sides. After we were in the air and at the cruising altitude, which meant the temperature in the plane dropped to subzero, we pulled our blankets or sleeping bags out and did anything we could to get warm. Chief; two of my team members, Ben and Levi; and I jumped into our sleeping bags and then got into our hammocks for the plane ride. The flight was fun. Since we were smashed in together, we swayed together like a Newton's cradle—one of those swinging ball things that you sometimes see on a businessman's desk. The other guys and I were very close together to keep warm, so when one person rolled over, we all had to roll over. At one time, Levi, one of my intel soldiers, had a minor mishap. He was sleeping next to me. He hadn't tied his hammock up correctly, and during our swaying, it broke free. His scream was hilarious, and then he was gone. Wrapped up in his cocoon and bundled up in his sleeping bag, he was lucky he didn't get hurt. We yelled at him for having left a gap, exposing Ben and me to the cold, and then helped him tie a proper knot. The flight was about ten hours to Germany. I think we slept for about half an hour of it.

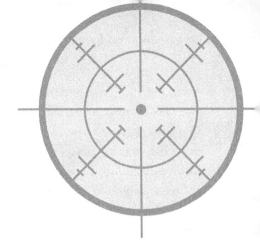

2

Germany—Ausfahrt!

> That there may be no division in the body, but that the members may have the same care for one another. If one member suffers, all suffer together; if one member is honored, all rejoice together.
>
> —1 Corinthians 12:25–26

We flew to Ramstein, Germany, where we had a twenty-four-hour layover. After we had disembarked, a couple of buses drove us to barracks where we were provided two rooms for housing with a couple of bunks and meager accommodations. I knew that I had a good group of guys when they asked if it would be cool if we shared a room together. I unrolled my sleeping bag on the floor, then Chief, Ben, Levi, and my civil affairs planning expert, Cece, unrolled their sleeping bags next to mine in the small room. After unloading our luggage, we decided to take advantage of our short break and explore our surroundings in Germany. We were able to walk down to a cafe, where we shared some coffee and discussed what attractions interested everyone in the group. Having plenty of time to kill, Chief spoke to the waitress and got us a cab that drove us to the post exchange, where we were able to take care of our essentials. We enjoyed some German food, grabbed some snacks from the little shop, and then wandered around grabbing things that we needed such as winter clothing for the next flight and ranger panties, because these short-shorts are extremely comfortable for working out. To pass whatever time remained, we met up at the movie theater in the mall. The only movie playing at the time was *Mission: Impossible.* My team huddled together inside the theater while Perry distributed a few beers, understanding that we had an exemption memorandum to the General Order No. 1, which prohibits alcohol on a deployment. We kicked back and watched Ethan Hunt save the world once again.

I know that I fell asleep, as did a couple of my guys, because the other captain with us decided to take a picture so that he would have something to hold over my head in case he needed it during the deployment to show we were drinking alcohol. This was not good for me, but it is a good memory. This was a great opportunity for my team to experience a little happiness and relaxation before we continued our journey. I believe that if I am going to require my guys to work hard, I have to provide them with an escape. However, I will not send them off into town without joining them. Given that we were representatives of the United States, I wanted to ensure that everyone behaved appropriately on our outings. We took time in Germany to center ourselves and bond in an attempt to show each other that even though we missed our families, we would make it through everything together. This time was not a party but was an opportunity to bond as a team and a moment to realize our deployment was starting.

After the movie and a few more German brats, we retired for the night. The next day we ate breakfast at the dining facility on base and then walked off post, finding a bus stop that took us into the local town. Seeing a castle on a hill, we walked up the huge mountain and soon found ourselves sitting on picnic tables, once again enjoying German food and each other's company while overlooking beautiful Germany with a historic castle behind us as a backdrop. Honestly, the twenty-four hours we had together in Germany was a great team-building time, and because of that time together, I will forever be endeared to my teammates and want to be close to them.

We walked back though the town to return to the base, stopping for lunch at a small-town cafe that was founded in 1738. Our meal consisted of schnitzel and bratwurst. Today was a rare occurrence in that we felt like tourists instead of soldiers. Finally, after making it back to our gear, we packed everything up and loaded onto the buses that would take us back to the plane. On the return trip to the bird, Cannon, one of our intel soldiers, stood up and yelled for the bus to stop. His supervisor asked what was going on, and he said that he had left his computer in the barracks. So, we paused the whole deployment and went back to get his computer before leaving again. This shows how important soldiers' equipment is, especially an intelligence analyst's computer. It was a great impression, you silly dude. The final leg of our journey was uneventful. Similar to the first leg, we slept until we landed at Baghdad International Airport.

3

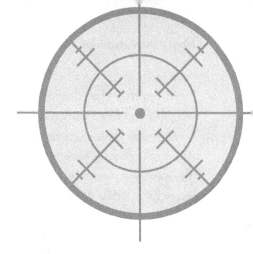

Iraq

Through one may be overpowered, two can defend
themselves. A cord of three strands is not quickly broken.

—Ecclesiastes 4:12

We disembarked after the plane landed and the doors opened. We
were happily greeted by the heat of Iraq, which allowed us to thaw
out from the freezing flight. We in-processed at the welcome desk,
signing into the country, and then waited around for a smaller plane
to take us the short distance to Erbil, Iraq.

Once we had landed in Erbil, our equipment was tossed into
a pickup truck. We jumped into a nasty van to drive to another
welcome center to log in. We were given the rules and were handed
our room keys. I felt like the luckiest man in the world because I
had been assigned a CHU (containerized housing unit), which is
a bedroom made from a shipping container, with Chief Mike. We
unloaded our equipment into a room that was smaller than our
accommodations back in Germany, and then we were given the
grand tour. We saw our office, which was in the same building as
the headquarters' tactical operation command center, located next

door to the gym. To all soldiers, a gym is the second-most important building after the dining facility. My civil affairs planning team would spend just as much time in the gym as we would the office. It was our way to unwind and relax after the long days we would have. About a mile away was the dining facility, which was good because, like most every man, we each ate a lot, so the walk to and from would burn the calories, which we counted as extra PT. The team that had been there before us consisted of three people. We replaced them with our team of nine, so things were going to be interesting for us. I don't really know what the people we replaced did, but I had great expectations of what we were going to accomplish.

Chief Michael explained our time in Iraq best, saying as follows:

> As an emerging and new capability to the unit, our civil affairs battalion (minus) had an incredibly unique mission. The team was made up of five different sections that had anywhere from one to three personnel per team. The intelligence team (Sergeant First Class Lee, Staff Sergeant Cannon, Sergeant Pierce) is self-explanatory as they conducted the intel portion, but even though it is self-explanatory, this does not take away from the importance they held for our mission. The operations team (Sergeant Perry, Captain Vogel, Captain Turnbull) led the daily updates and battle rhythm for the other teams to ensure our focus stayed on point. The geospatial intelligence (Sergeant Connley) team focused on imaging for operations and intelligence, as well as geographic maps and inputs for forward teams for a better view of the area of operations. The Human Terrain Analysis (HNA) (Sergeant First Class Cece) team focused on the human networking in and around the regions where teams were collecting data and intel. During this process, a certain software

was used to determine how many connections are made through different villages and cities. By using this process, the teams were able to look at a map of the network and leverage certain groups or individuals to get information and other resources. The targeting team (Chief Warrant Officer 2 Reese) was responsible for integration, planning, and coordination of the army's targeting methodology as a component of conducting civil military operations to analyze human networks and civil vulnerabilities within the CENTCOM [US Central Command] area of responsibility (the Middle East). By interfacing and coordinating targeting and intelligence efforts with CENTCOM intelligence staff and other US intelligence agencies, we were able to provide important detailed information to other members of our team. The targeting team was also responsible for maintaining intelligence estimates for seven countries within the CENTCOM AOR [area of responsibility] and provided targeting expertise to the staff and our team members on the ground in the forward area of operations.

I could not have said it better myself.

The first day we were on the ground, I had to attend an evening debriefing where every department head briefed the commander on what had occurred with respect to his or her department. I was ready to jump into the hot seat, so I joined the soldier whom I would be replacing. Standing in front of the entire tactical operations center (TOC), I was excited because before the soldier I was replacing introduced me, the commander of operations stood up and said, "Jonathan Turnbull? I remember you from West Point. What? Like, ten years ago?!" I blushed, thinking that I must have been a very bad cadet for the commander to have remembered me. I certainly remembered him! Colonel Jeff, also known as "Twerp" by a select few, is one of those individuals whom everyone knew back then, and even now everyone in the army knows him if you mention his name. It was an honor to be remembered as I have always looked up to this man. We told him about the current atmosphere in Syria with regard to civil considerations, and we briefed him on operations that civil affairs had conducted, before being dismissed with a hand wave, an "Okay," and a "Welcome to the war."

Over the next month, I would work directly for the S3, a colonel named Ben. He was by far one of the smartest individuals I have ever met, and he trusted his subordinates, which was incredible. I loved working for him. Command operations had decided to use us because when they needed the information, they expected us to have it—and they supported us all the way. One day when we were briefing the general in charge about the whole Middle East, a question was directed at my lowest-ranking soldier. A couple of higher-ranking officers dismissed him. Colonel Jeff shut everyone up and turned to the soldier, named Connley. Not only was he the lowest-ranking member on our team, but also he was possibly the lowest-ranking individual in Erbil, Iraq. Colonel Jeff heard every word of Connley's answer and then told the whole world that we were going to do exactly what Connley had recommended. This was not a single occurrence; it happened often. Colonel Jeff stood behind me on multiple occasions and would support me even against my own leadership. I greatly respect him and was proud to call him my boss. He was the first leader whom I called my friend, and he was one whom I would fight to work for no matter what, even if I had to brew coffee or clean toilets.

Speaking of toilets, Colonel Jeff had one of the most amazing signs hanging above his toilets. In the Middle East, you must not flush toilet paper for any reason. We carried around Ziplock baggies and would use them to throw away our dirty toilet paper. I am pretty sure that is why there will always be war in the Middle East, but whatever. Using Colonel Jeff's bathroom one day, I saw a sign above his toilet that read, "Do not throw away toilet paper in the toilet. The only thing that belongs in the toilet is your hopes, dreams, tears, ambitions, and such." I thought that was pretty incredible.

Every Sunday, Colonel Jeff and Command Sergeant Major Frank, another individual who demanded respect and had excellence pouring through his veins, would hold a little physical exertion event called a "Sunday Fun Day." Sounds amazing, right? There was nothing fun about it. It was very enjoyable getting together with the high-caliber, highly tuned individuals on the compound. Accomplishing a physical task that was impossible for a human being, one that probably would have made Spartans crinkle their noses at the prospect of attempting, became a weekly goal. I tried to erase any of these workouts from my memory, but if I may try to impress you here, I will mention that one day Colonel Jeff made us do one hundred pull-ups along with a million double-unders. This requires jumping rope with two passes per jump instead of just one. I love working out and never turn down the opportunity, but whatever these were, they were not workouts. I would grab my team to work out every day. I was not the kind of leader who demanded my soldiers sit behind their computers and wait for an email, so we worked out, networked, and enjoyed midnight chow.

Midnight chow might have been one of the most amazing things about Erbil. A young man there cooked pancakes that were so memorable that once I eventually made it to Syria, I asked my guys to take pictures of the pancakes and send them to me. Our routine ended up having us work out around 2200 and then grab midnight chow pancakes after a shower, before calling it a night and quickly calling back home. I was blessed that none of my guys came back the size of a hippo.

My guys impressed me with how much work they accomplished in the first two weeks. We worked more than twelve hours per day providing relevant information to the commander, in return receiving plenty of "attaboys," one of the highest forms of praise in the community. To prevent my gents from burning themselves out,

I threw them into a van at one point in the second week and took them on a surprise trip. Iraq was much different from anything they could remember from previous deployments. We drove in a soft-shelled vehicle through the gates. I drove us around town before stopping at Ace Hardware. Everyone walked around the hardware store letting off some steam and rejuvenating themselves, just feeling as if they were back home. We bought some spray paint for our guns, along with other odds and ends. I then drove us to a steakhouse called DC Steakhouse, which had been recommended by some of the guys on base. While some of the guys ordered $100 steaks, I ordered everyone some local food. While eating, we enjoyed a singer whose voice was as beautiful as she was. I rounded the adventure off with a sweet treat at a gelato shop (where we got some of the sweet frozen treat) that would become known to us as the most important location in Iraq. On the drive back to base, I was able to talk about the day's events. I compared it to the importance of civil affairs operations during wartime. We were walking around town eating memorable treats and driving a regular vehicle in a country torn up after decades of war. Upon returning to base, I found that I had successfully recharged everyone's batteries. Then we got back into the fight. I always make sure to take care of not only my soldiers but also myself. I think it is something every army officer should do with his or her subordinates. Reflecting on who I am and where I am keeps me sane. When I have any downtime, my thoughts, of course, are always on my family—Samantha and Ian—before anyone else. Samantha and I have not had a good run as husband and wife. I know that the fault for this is mine, and I continually pray that I will be able to be the husband she deserves. Deployments are hard no matter how amazing of a wife she is. I look for any opportunity to show her how much I appreciate her. The first week in Iraq, I found a good opportunity, although it was probably a really bad idea, to demonstrate my love for her. There was a Kurdish tattoo shop about fifty feet from my CHU. After much deliberation, I paid the artist for a band around my right forearm with my and Sarah's wedding anniversary date in roman numerals as the highlight. After I'd gotten the tattoo, my boss Colonel Jeff took the opportunity to let me know in front of everyone that many soldiers who had gotten tattoos here had gotten hepatitis A. He said that I needed to get checked immediately. After sweating though my clothes, I found out that he was only joking with me, which I found funny. I appreciated his humor. I will always have my anniversary printed in my skin so I don't forget it, but now the joke is on me. Also, I will always remember the only other officer besides me with a sense of humor, the one who told me I had hepatitis A from getting a tattoo in Iraq.

4

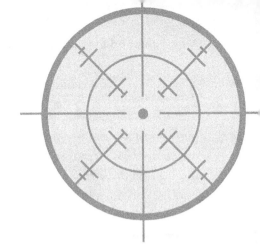

Syria

By wisdom a house is built, and by understanding
it is established; by knowledge the rooms are
filled with all precious and pleasant riches.

—Proverbs 24:3–4

In the army, we soldiers do as we are told—most of the time. In late
September of 2018 when I prepared to brief Colonel Jeff, he stopped
me before I started. "Jon, I need help. Come up here."

Jeff needs help from me? Sweating, I walked around the computers
and the people, going up to my boss's computer. "Yes, sir? I live to
serve." I hoped he noted my sarcasm. Looking at me standing over
his computer, while he was reading what I guessed was an email, he
said, "I need a team leader for a cross-functional teams in Syria. I
also need a civil affairs kind of person to join the team with multiple
Special Forces soldiers, psyops soldiers, and civilians who are experts
on the region. Can you make a recommendation?" My heart was
racing.

"Yes, sir. My team will do some military decision-making
and will run it through Colonel Ben, and then I will make a

recommendation." He nodded. I returned to my spot in the TOC (tactical operations center). After a couple of days and a lot more information about what the TOC actually needed, I and my team presented four courses of action to the commander. The mission was to deny ISIS the freedom to move by empowering or enhancing the legitimacy of the local government to rule in the eyes of the Iraqi people. I could go; Vogel, the other captain, could go; Cece, our most experienced NCO, could go; and Chief Mike could go. Colonel Jeff said that the choice already had been made the day he asked and that I needed to be on a bird that night. I had been chosen by the commander to join Team Manbij. I was extremely honored. When I first met Colonel Jeff while at West Point, I wanted one day to work for him. This was an opportunity that I had always dreamed of but never knew would be a possibility. I packed my bags, knowing this would be the most important thing I had ever done in my life. I could not let Colonel Jeff down.

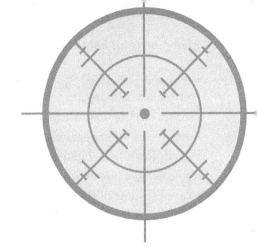

5

A New Place

Blessed shall you be in the city, and blessed
shall you be in the country.

—Deuteronomy 28:3

Where in the world was I? The drive from the Special Operations Command Center for Syria to KLZ (Kobani Landing Zone) East, a US military airport in the middle of Syria, where the commander of civil affairs operations was located, was an uneventful ride. I enjoyed my company with my new team sergeant and looked forward to spending time with this individual. His name was Justin. I knew that he was a very intelligent and driven individual and that I had a great opportunity to glean more information from him than a person could get from many years of college. As we crossed the Euphrates River, he told me about how the Turks had conducted a military operation at this exact spot. The goal was to remove a historic religious relic before ISIS was able to destroy it. Down the river there was an Ottoman castle that remained from the Crusades. This land was tantalizing to me because I loved history. Here I was not only walking the land where history came alive but also was going to be a part of history, a part of an operation to remove an evil that plagued this region. Driving up a bank from the Euphrates, Justin showed me holes in the road where, he said, an ISIS convoy had been halted during a coalition operation many years back and coalition air assets rained down a molten-lead death upon the terrorist organization, also leaving a lasting impression on the terrain. On the sides of the road were some of the vehicles that had been crippled beyond repair, burnt-out shapes and shells reminiscent of their previous lives. This gave me a perspective on the phrase *war torn*. I was grateful for the demonstration because, through it, I gained a deeper appreciation for what the people of our area of operations (AO) had endured over the past decade, which renewed my vigor to eliminate the infection plaguing these innocent people. Justin pointed out a large group of buildings in the distance, off at about eleven o'clock, when we were about five miles away. "There, sir, is where you will be living. We call our home the Tay-Tay Memorial Grain Silo (named after none other than the famous Taylor Swift herself). Welcome home."

I grew excited as we drove closer and started taking a few pictures with my phone. After we exited the traffic circle that was outside our compound and prepared to enter our walled-in compound, I saw that one of the buildings had a giant hole in the center of it. We passed through two gates, and then another, to enter our motor pool, where we parked the vehicles. Justin grabbed my bags and helped me carry them up the two flights of stairs to the second wooden door on the left. The door had my name on a piece of paper with "Civil Affairs" written on it. This would be my room for the next six months. Justin told me to download my gear and said that he would return later for dinner. Again, he welcomed me home with a hug. Out of habit from the last four years of repeated deployments, I dropped my clothes on my bed, along with my pillow and my sleeping bag. As I had learned during my time at West Point, I pulled out my shoes and lined them up under my cot. The toes of my shoe were aligned in "dress right, dress" order—in other words, in a straight line—so when I got out of bed, I could slide a pair out and throw them on without much effort.

I propped my rifle up next to my door with the handle facing me and then sat down on my bed, waiting for something to happen. Not being a patient individual, I debated whether to wait for Justin or go off by myself. I decided to wait. I didn't know if there were things hidden around the compound that would make for a nasty surprise to an unsuspecting individual. Even though I was observant, I didn't want to miss something and accidently hit a booby trap. Soon, after sending off a group text message to my family saying that I was safe and at my new home, there was a knock on the door, and the door opened a crack. A young man entered and introduced himself as Nick. He was a psyops soldier who lived in the room next to mine. He asked if I wanted a tour. We were soon wandering around the compound.

I was thrilled to see that we had probably one of the best gyms that I have ever seen on a deployment. We had multiple squat racks and enough weights to destroy even the largest lifter. Nick showed me where the bathroom was; it was probably the nicest bathroom in all of Syria, with multiple European toilets and individual showers. Nick informed me that the building we were occupying was once one of the largest grain factories in Syria. The company was German owned, and our building had ten floors. Our vehicles were kept on the first floor. During the battle to remove ISIS from the silo, we dropped multiple large bombs on the facility. A large part of the building collapsed in the middle, which I learned was what I had seen when we drove up. Nick said that two additional bunker-buster bombs didn't explode and were currently sitting harmlessly in the basement. That piqued my interest. Now I wanted to see the basement. Nick showed me our TOC, where our planning and controls would be conducted.

After Nick ran out of things to show me, he passed me off to a well-built individual named Kyle. Kyle, a weapons specialist, was known as a Bravo. He oversaw security throughout the compound and for the team. He walked me around, showing each of the four battle positions. We discussed what I was capable of. I tried to impress him, but he saw right through me. He instantly pointed out that the reflex sight on my Glock was mounted incorrectly. I chuckled about it; he had me there. But if we could shoot, I told him, I would show him what I could do, rather than just *tell* him what I could do. He was a great individual. I tried to get him to be part of every mission I went on. I respected him and knew that he was not only competent but also capable. One of my favorite conversations I had while in Syria was with Kyle, while we waited for the team leader, who was in a key leader engagement.

Kyle and I sat outside talking with some of the local people drinking some gross apple drinks and found out quickly about an ISIS plot to attack coalition forces. Kyle remained cool, calm, and collected the whole time, yet I was very excited. I calmed down quickly when our hosts, the local military, brought us food. The only other fascinating thing about our housing location was that we shared it with the Manbij Military Council (MMC). There was a military hospital on our compound. If any of our partner force soldiers were wounded, they would be sent there. There was also a jailhouse that housed a few ISIS fighters whom supposedly ISIS had tried to free a few days before I showed up. I loved my new home and saw it as a castle that we would defend to the last. It would be a beacon of hope and a symbol of freedom in the region.

Nick, who had showed me around, honored me later during my deployment by asking me to reenlist him. We conducted his ceremony on top of our building overlooking the city of Manbij, in the face of ISIS. With Old Glory as our backdrop, he raised his right hand and stated, "I promise to support and defend the Constitution of the United States of America against all enemies, foreign and domestic; to bear true faith and allegiance to the same; and to obey the orders of the president of the United States and officers appointed over him, according to the regulations and the Uniform Code of Military Justice, so help me God!" I shook his hand and told everyone who was standing there as witnesses that he had reenlisted to show his patriotism, valor, and loyalty. His demonstration brought tears to my eyes and honored me. I viewed this as the single most important thing I could do as an officer in the military. Thank you, Nick!

During the ceremony, I had a pleasant flashback to another time when I had been honored in such a way. While in Afghanistan in 2012, I had the opportunity to stand on a Russian tank, destroyed decades before, facing one of my incredible soldiers, Staff Sergeant Jay. This was on top of the tank, right next to our combat outpost on the northern border with Tajikistan. As had been the case in Syria, we had the US flag behind us. Sergeant Jay had reenlisted for enough time to make it to twenty years in the military and his retirement. I didn't have a beard in Afghanistan, but my smile stretched from ear to ear because of the happiness I felt standing in the face of our enemy. I hadn't had a tank to stand on in Syria, but the feeling of happiness was similar. Nick's reenlistment is another memory I will savor my entire life.

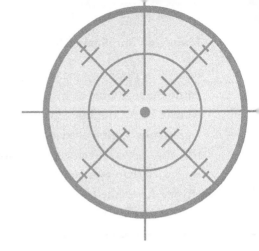

6

Meeting a Princess

She opens her mouth with wisdom, and the
teaching of kindness is on her tongue.

—Proverbs 31:26

Walking around our base the first night in Syria, I was exploring just for fun. I walked to the back of the grain silo. Sitting there, huddled around a small green plastic table, were three of our linguists. They were snacking on some bread, drinking tea, smoking a hookah, and laughing noisily. Seeing me materialize out of the shadows, the linguist named Ghadir invited me to join the group. I sat down with them, excited to practice my very poor Arabic and hoping to get to know these individuals who had always impressed me.

After introductions and a little small talk, Ghadir let me know that she was an immigrant from Syria. Her family had moved to Atlanta when she was three years old. Her real name was Ghadir Tahir, but she went by Jasmine or Princess Jasmine, or Yaz for short. She wanted to help her native country, but not through violence, which is why she had become a linguist. The other two interpreters, Ali and Jad, had similar stories. I count them as equals. Ghadir quickly became my preferred linguist because she opened up an entire demographic of people whom we couldn't talk to without a woman being around.

Ghadir Tahir looked just like a Disney princess. I could instantly tell why she was so respected for who she was. She knew more about this place than everyone else and had more tenure than just about anyone here. She cooked dinner on this day. After we had eaten some goat meat seasoned with salt and pepper, with a side dish of rice and corn, Ghadir did something that surprised me by asking me if I wanted to do anything in particular. Thinking of the scene from *Beauty and the Beast*, I replied that I wanted to go to the "West Wing," which we knew was forbidden. In this case, I was Belle. "Yes, ma'am, I want to see the basement." After having heard some rumors and seen a picture in the TOC, I knew there was a bomb down there. I had to lay my eyes on it. Ghadir nodded and led me outside and around the kitchen, where we disposed of our dishes, and then walked up a flimsy ladder. I followed. Toward the back of the building, I saw where the bomb had torn half of it away. It was growing dark out, and since most of this part of the building was destroyed, I turned the light of my rifle on so we didn't get hurt and followed Ghadir through the rubble, down a flight of stairs, and into a good-sized room. I almost lost my breath when she turned to face me and sat down on the ground, on what looked to be a large green pencil. "Um, Ghadir, is that the …?" I trailed off as a smile split her face, probably because she was watching me fumble for words. I paused where I was and then turned my flashlight up toward the ceiling, where I saw a hole the size of a projectile. This was where the bomb had come through the building.

"This bomb came from the sky," Ghadir said. I wanted to tell her, *No duh.* "I guess they didn't set the depth right, so it didn't explode like the one in the middle, which blew up the rest of this building. The same thing happened to the one below where we live. The whole story of these bombs is kind of sad." She patted the bomb while she spoke, making me cringe a little. I still get goose bumps thinking about that place.

"ISIS used this compound as one of their headquarters. As the SDF [Syrian Democratic Forces] tried to take it, ISIS ran up to the roof and sniped innocent people. The coalition dropped a few big bombs on the roof. The bombs drove the ISIS guys inside. This happened multiple times, each episode within a few months of the one just previous. Finally, some of the leadership got sick and tired of our guys attacking the building and of ISIS going to the roof. The bombs and ISIS were pushing our guys out, so we dropped these bad boys on the building to destroy it, which only partially worked. I will show you later, but beneath us are a lot of tunnels, and as these big bombs crashed through the building, ISIS went into the tunnels for protection. Unbeknownst to ISIS, we knew where the exits were. Coalition had blocked all the exits, having come in here and blocked these ones too. Then they tried to clear out the tunnels, but ISIS was too strong and killed too many of our guys, so we just sat tight and waited for ISIS to surrender. I think it took three days. They surrendered because they were dehydrated. It was a really bad way for them to go, but honestly, after everything evil they have done in the area, I don't think there are many people who mourned them."

This was an interesting glimpse of a woman whom I would take as my primary linguist. She was a lioness who, I saw, had a tender heart but she also had a ferocious side. She was someone whom I could take with me anywhere and would not have to protect her because I knew she could hold her own.

Throughout my time in Syria, I spent more time with Ghadir than with anyone else. She became just like a sister to me. She was an invaluable member of the team, especially when we would challenge our partner force to a game of volleyball. Don't get me wrong, she was not any good at volleyball, but when we destroyed the other team, she would smooth over the situation and make sure there were no conflicts between anyone.

Ghadir was more than a linguist; she was also a cultural adviser.

My mission was to build up the local government to delegitimize ISIS in the area. On one of the most important missions early in the deployment, I had to gain the trust of a local leader and leverage his influence. I told this to my team, and we went to the civil administration. Honoring local custom, the city administrator offered us coffee and tea. After drinking the "Kurdish" coffee and talking shop, Ghadir flipped her coffee cup upside down on the platter, spilling the coffee grounds all over the place. I got really upset. Seeing that I was about to say something, she held up her hand, motioning me to stay calm and to trust her. I thought we were in trouble, convinced that this relationship was about to be destroyed. This goes to show what I knew, because when the administrator walked in, he took note of the upturned coffee cup Ghadir had lifted toward him as she asked, "Can you read my fortune?" The administrator beamed with a broad smile and did just that while cleaning up the mess. Leaving Syria, I reflected that this was by far the strongest relationship that we had. I knew that I could return to the area and have unlimited access to this individual and his influence.

7

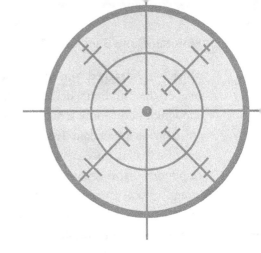

No Girls Allowed

> Speak up for those who cannot speak for themselves,
> for the rights of all you are destitute.
>
> —Proverbs 31:8

Reflecting on our team's accomplishments, I cannot think of anything more notable than what we did for the future of Syria. Early into my deployment, I was allowed inside many of the more reputable schools in the region. Teams before me had already turned Ramadan Hiju Primary School back into a beacon of education from the ISIS jailhouse and torture building it had been. To continue providing legitimacy to the government, I thought bolstering the education system would deliver the best bang for the buck.

While we were walking through another school, Ghadir, whispering, informed us, "The government is taking us to a boys-only school." To my shame, I had not noticed this. I poked my head into the nearest classroom to validate this claim. I asked the teacher in rough Arabic, and she told me that there were only boys at this school.

Upon hearing this, Scotty, Ghadir, and I grabbed our government official and dragged him into a vacant room. Sitting him down in one of the children's desks, I asked him bluntly, "Why are you showing us boys-only schools? Why are girls not allowed here?"

Obviously shaken from my direct questioning, or possibly because I had once again drawn my pistol as a precaution, he responded, "This is not just a boys' school. Girls are not permitted to attend school. Three months ago, a young woman was in school here when an ISIS man found her. He dragged her out of the classroom into the courtyard and shot her, throwing her body into the fountain in the center of the courtyard as an example to others that girls were not allowed to learn. We thanked him for his time and returned to our base immediately. Working with the State Department, the Department of Defense, the Syrian Democratic Forces, and the civil administration of Manbij, our team made a plan to ensure the return of all the girls to school. Many military members scoffed at this plan, calling it too humanitarian, but we held true. My team kept the faith, knowing that this operation would serve to accomplish a far greater strategic mission objective than minor lethal strikes.

At the end of the month there was a Syrian Democratic Forces soldier in each school providing security, and the girls flooded the education system. So many girls returned to school that we had to work with Syrian engineers to build temporary classrooms around the city. In one town to the north called Dadat, four thousand young girls who did not get to attend school for seven years while ISIS was in charge are today still in school. This operation was such a success that children everywhere, when they saw our team, would run up to us and give us high fives and hugs to Ghadir or Shannon. One young woman thanked me for protecting her at school and then asked if I could protect her at home from a really mean man. Scotty was so excited to hear this that we got a follow-on lethal mission, one that had spurred from this seemingly humanitarian mission. At the end of the day, it was through this school mission that we were able to map out the entire ISIS network in our sector, not through any other means.

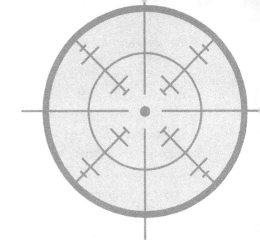

8

The Hydroelectric Dam and Those Hydroelectric Dam People

Whoever believes in me, as Scripture has said, rivers of living waters will flow from within them.

—John 7:38

One morning shortly after I arrived in Syria, I heard a very authoritative knock on my bedroom door. I rolled over, murmuring, "One second." I looked at my watch, grimacing because it was only six o'clock in the morning. Jumping from my cot after I had unzipped my sleeping bag, I lifted the latch and swung open the door. Standing there directly in front of me was Ghadir. Her hair was dripping wet; her lips were quivering and blue. I tucked my pistol in my front pocket and followed Ghadir down the wide hallway toward the tactical operations center (TOC). She stopped at the door and turned to face me wearing her usual smile. It was a look that I knew well. I also knew it was dangerous because it was the kind of look that got her whatever she wanted.

"Jon, I just finished working out, and when I went downstairs to take a shower, there wasn't any electricity," she stated. Looking around I didn't notice that the lights were out. Our lights were always out to maintain security. Ghadir then pleaded for me to get the power turned on, not for light, but for the water heaters. Processing everything slower than normal, probably because of the fact that it was early in the morning, I realized that Ghadir believed there was a crisis because we didn't have electricity for hot showers.

This interaction created a mission focus that had us visit a power relay station inside the city. After an hour's drive to a spot south of our base, I sat on a very uncomfortable sofa, flanked by Ghadir and the government administrator who had read her fortune. We were in deep conversation while drinking coffee, with another focus on how I could continue to providing legitimacy for the government. I drifted off rather than focusing on the Arabic. After all, when I went through my language courses after I had been selected for civil affairs, I learned an old dialect of Arabic that is used mostly for prayers and reading the Koran but not for modern conversations. I was learning conversational Arabic from Ghadir, but I trusted her completely in the conversation, hoping to empower her to manage the relationships we were creating since she was the cultural expert. I could only pick up a couple of words in every dialogue. Ghadir let me know that the administrator said the government was not receiving power so could not distribute it, which is what had led us to this spot.

The Tishrin Hydroelectric Dam is located on the Euphrates River in the heart of Syria. During the war against ISIS, coalition forces bombed the dam, so I went there, first and foremost, to assess the level of damage. I wanted to fix whatever the problem was so we could restore power, which would allow Ghadir to shower, along with four hundred thousand other people. Our guide led us through a maze of rooms. Before I knew it, we were standing in a pitch-black room that was very damp. "This room is where the water enters and spins the fans before it exits," our guide said. We stood ten feet from the main door. I saw why we didn't have much power: there was no water flowing through any of the rooms.

I lifted my voice, asking, "So why isn't there water in here?"

The administrator turned to face me as he answered, "There is a signed agreement between Turkey, Syria, and Iraq that all countries will have five hundred cubic meters of water flow per second through the Euphrates River. All of the dams are planned around this; however, the Turks have hindered this flow to only two hundred. I will show you the flow rate from each day if you would like. Can you do something for us?" I smiled at the man, knowing that he had just given me a golden nugget. I knew exactly who could try to render aid.

The rest of the tour was very impressive. I took notes of any areas for which the coalition could provide specialized engineering support, which in turn would benefit the people and enhance the war effort. The administrator gave me the statics before we left. The conversation back home evolved around how we could help and if it was something we even wanted to attempt.

The following day, I got to work and contacted multiple government offices and agencies that I had used on previous deployments, but at the end of the day, I received the most beneficial help from my civil affairs planning teams, notably from Specialist Connley, who was back in Iraq. After much heartache from my immediate boss—I had gone over his head because he was dragging his feet—I got the solution. I decided to use my West Point degree as a geographic information scientist / mapmaker. Understanding the usefulness and importance of maps, I reached out to Connley. Taking a page out of what I had learned about leadership from Colonel Jeff, I knew the best way forward and how to solve this problem, namely, by consulting and trusting the experts. We ended up getting a volume assessment of a lake above a dam in Turkey. It showed that the Turks were preventing the maximum flow of water into Syria. The civil affairs planning team did a nice write-up for me using many big words. I passed the report along to the State Department for use. From flash to bang, identifying the problem to the water flowing at full rate had taken less than one month. God bless the United States' State Department.

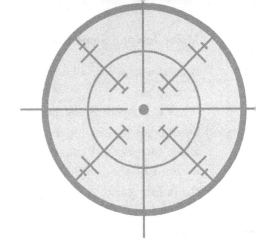

9

Hamar Labdee Clinic

I have given you authority to trample on snakes and scorpions and
to overcome all the power of the enemy; nothing will harm you.

—Luke 10:19

I prized the fact that my team was one of the only elements within
the area that maintained unlimited mobility—just like the other
cross-functional teams in Syria. We held legitimate reasons for our
travel, which were almost always centered on humanitarian causes.
Back in October was one such mission, the first one I had been on
during this deployment. Four trucks were driving along the border
to ensure ease of access for our coalition partners and also to ensure
the population was safe and secure so we could continue providing
legitimacy for the local government. I told the team that we would
visit multiple medical centers along the border today to assess them,
adding that we would stop to talk with any villagers we saw. As
we drove, I noted in my notebook every important place along a
military grid site that I would later report to my chain of command
as a no-fire location. A no-fire location is always an important spot

such as a school or a hospital that coalition forces respect and will protect.

We stopped at the first medical center, which overlooked a border-crossing site for the Syrian regime and potentially for their allies, such as the Russians. After pulling off the road and parking in front of the building's eight-foot wall, Ghadir walked inside the building with a couple of soldiers from the Syrian Democratic Forces. I quickly ran through the duties and responsibilities of each member present today. While I was asking some of the guys to get an approximate layout drawing of the center, Ghadir reappeared in an opening of the wall. Her face was beaming, and her smile split her face in half. Her shoulders were slightly hunched forward, and she had her arms wrapped around a bundle of blankets. As she approached our vehicles, much to everyone's surprise, she notified us, "Just so everyone knows and isn't surprised, the building is occupied by refugees such as this little baby." She finished speaking by holding the bundle of blankets up for us to see the little baby.

As I followed her back into the clinic, I saw that there were about twenty squatters living in there. Sitting down on the ground with an older gentleman, I drank the steaming tea offered and thanked them, asking, "Can you tell me who you are and how you came to be here?"

The elderly gentleman at first seemed hesitant to answer my question, but after we had talked back and forth about the importance of family and how I had a son the same age as one of the little ones running around the clinic, he opened up and informed me that his family had immigrated to this place from the regime-controlled area. He blessed me and my team for making the area safe for his family and offered any bits of information I might need.

I took his information down in my notebook and made sure that I sent up a contact report to the State Department requesting support for the refugees. It took the State Department less than a month to relocate the family to a better place, one where the children could attend school. As soon as this was completed, I was able to work with the local government and fully outfit the clinic with medical equipment so that it could help the nearly five thousand people living along the border there.

Following our stop at the clinic with the refugees living in it, we drove a short distance to the next town along the border. I was still mapping out the human terrain, getting a good understanding of where we stood in the eyes of the population and what the disposition was of the enemy population. The next town had a medical clinic in it as well, which we pulled up to just as we had done at the refugee clinic. Next to this clinic was a large compound with a man sitting in front. Wearing a uniform, he had a gun resting comfortably in his lap. We called that out quickly. One of my soldiers had a gun trained on him before I stepped out of my vehicle and covered the individual the entire time I visited the clinic. Ham (the team's medic who was assigned to us for the day), Ghadir, and I walked into the clinic and were met quickly by three nurses, who excitedly asked us what we were doing. We found out that the compound next door was an SDF (Syrian Democratic Forces) police station and that we were mostly safe. The nurses took us into their office and served us tea, as is customary. While drinking the steaming liquid, I introduced myself and my team and got buy-in from the nurses by asking who they were and how their families were doing. Before too long I had asked the few questions that I found were customary, and which it never hurt to ask, but today these questions had profound results. The answer to one such question blew me away: "Are we safe here today?" As I asked it, the head nurse shook her head back and forth. I immediately turned and looked at Ghadir, assuming I had spoken incorrectly even though I had practiced these questions with her thousands of times and she said I had developed a Syrian-sounding accent. Seeing her smile fade, and watching her put her tea down with shaky hands, I keyed the mic on my radio and called for our head of security, who was also our token Navy SEAL, Scott. "Scotty, we might need you in here."

"Roger. On the way," his voice crackled through the radio.

Ghadir was speaking with the nurses in a low voice. I couldn't catch what they were saying.

"Ghadir," I said. "Ghadir!" I said again, this time with more authority in my voice. The second time quieted the room. She turned her head, scowled at me, and stood up. At this point, Scott came lumbering into the room, gun in hand and ready to fight. Ghadir strolled across the room and began talking quietly at me. I asked her to talk loud enough for everyone to hear since it was a danger everyone would face and I didn't like secrets. She nodded. "The head nurse says that there is an issue and that they have locked it in the bathroom."

I chuckled and stood up. "Can she take us to said bathroom, please?" Ghadir nodded and presented my inquiry to the nurse, whom we followed around the corner.

Scotty fell in beside me. "Sir, what's going on?"

I shrugged my shoulders and mumbled, "I don't know. She said there is a problem that she has locked in the bathroom here. Probably a clogged toilet that wouldn't flush or something." Chuckling to himself, Scotty pulled out his suppressor and started screwing it on his pistol. I eyeballed him.

Seeing my gaze, he told me, "You can't be too careful with these Syrians."

The nurse continued to talk with Ghadir. They stopped in front of a narrow white door.

Ghadir turned to face us. "She says this is a woman's bathroom and she doesn't want you gentlemen looking inside because it is inappropriate." Scotty then did something that I should have scolded him for, but it was something that I will always remember and something that I respect him for. Many times, we had taken Ghadir out to the back part of the compound and worked with her on marksmanship just in case we needed her in a firefight. This looked like it might be one of those cases.

Scotty tossed his gun in the air, catching it backward, and presented it to her handle first. "Ghadir, here. One is in the chamber.

Remember what we taught you about the fundamentals of shooting: trigger squeeze, side alignment, and breathe. We are right here, and we have your back."

The nurse pulled a good number of keys from her pocket and unlocked the door. I leaned against the wall, trying to see inside, while holding my pistol just in case, knowing I should have been getting more information and calling this up so everyone knew what was going on. The team was a few feet away, chatting while observing everything, ready to act. I quickly drew my pistol and stepped toward Ghadir. She let out a shriek and lifted Scotty's pistol, discharging a round into the bathroom with a sharp crack. Then I saw something that nightmares are made from. I did not expect to encounter a twenty-foot snake that had scaled the bathroom wall and was hanging from the ceiling like the snake in *The Jungle Book*. Ghadir had shot true. That large snake dropped to the ground with a sickening thud that still, to this day, makes me want to vomit. Scotty was instantly behind me, ready for action and, like me, dry-heaving.

Although each of us had forced back the urge to vomit, I almost lost it when one of the guys had to say that he wanted to grab the snake because, as a Special Forces (SF) soldier, he was a snake-eater. Scotty improved the mood when he followed that up with, "We need to do something because, as we all know, where there is one clogged toilet, there is always another." He said he would go and grab one of his grenades so we could drop it down the sewer hole. I told him no. The last thing I wanted was to have to clean sanitation from the whole building since blowing up the clogged toilet would just send sewage all over. Scotty smiled at that. At the end of the day, we didn't kill any more snakes. And we didn't take that snake home for the SF guys to eat. Additionally, none of the police came over to investigate why there had been a gunshot at the medical clinic, which was not a good sign of safety and security in the area.

After the ISIS snake episode, I conducted a quick assessment of the facility and found one more thing intriguing. After determining that the clinic needed a generator, some ultrasound machines, and basic medical equipment, I started writing everything up and asked what the name of the clinic was. The nurses shrugged their shoulders and said they didn't know. According to the map, the town's name was something like Hamar Labdee, but they didn't even know this. We laughed at the fact that people working in the clinic didn't know the name of their own town.

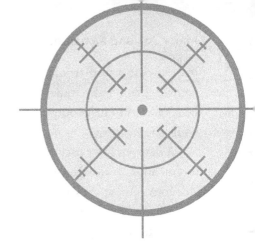

10

Zoe's Movie

Therefore encourage one another and build
one another up, just as you are doing.

—1 Thessalonians 5:11

At West Point Military Academy, I was told that we live for one reason, and that is to inspire those around us. No matter what we do, we will inspire everyone around us. It is our choice if we do so in a positive or a negative manner. What impact have you made on those around you?

Ghadir left our compound to go on vacation at the end of November, but before she left, I drove her to the flight line. "Jon, I wanted to let you know something that no one knows." She told me as we bounced along the dirt road to KLZ, "I do not have any intention of returning to Syria after my vacation." I almost slammed on the brakes of my SUV in reaction to the wind being knocked out of my lungs.

"I have half a mind to turn this truck around, Ghadir, and never let you leave, young lady," I responded with great effort since I had just had the wind knocked out of me. I was happy for her to be able to go home to spend time with her family, but I was also very upset that she hadn't told us sooner that she was leaving. I knew no matter what that we would remain friends and would always keep in contact. I could also understand why she didn't want to come back here. We said our goodbyes. I hoped she would change her mind while she was away.

As soon as I was back to our compound at the Tay-Tay Memorial Grain Silos, I knocked on Ghadir's door, hoping her roommate Zoe, our combat camera specialist, was present. Zoe was one of the best people I knew when it came to technological prowess. Much to my relief, she was present. I informed her of what Ghadir had told me and asked her to help me do something to get Ghadir to come back. Zoe said that she had a solution. That night, while I sat with my really good friends around the hookah lounge, Zoe walked up to us. She was always a wonder with a contagious smile on her face that rubbed off on us, so we enjoyed her presence. She said that she was putting together a short video for Ghadir and wanted to record us saying what impact she had made on us. Zoe got to work right away with her professional equipment.

I think the overall message that we compiled and sent to Ghadir was one of love, respect, and hope for her return. I attribute the success of my team to her actions and her knowledge. One thing that she did impart to me was her way of speaking Arabic. Once I was back stateside, I continued to study and speak Arabic; however, people I try speaking to often tell me that I sound like a Syrian from Damascus. I wear this badge with honor, thanks to Ghadir.

To make a long story short, the inspiration Ghadir brought to the team and the professionalism and actions of Zoe led to a quick run to the flight line a month later, where we picked up Ghadir from amidst the transients' tents to take her back home to our compound. While I carried one of her many bags to my truck, she confided in me, saying, "Jon, I don't want people to think I came back because of money or anything like that. I came back because I want to complete what we have started."

As a captain in the US Army, I always commanded each of my soldiers to inspire those around them. Dare to inspire.

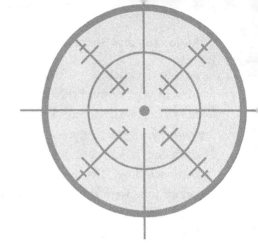

11

Lambchop,
a.k.a. Lamby

The Lord is good to all, and his mercy is over all that he has made.

—Psalm 145:9

Love on the battlefield is something that is misconstrued in movies. Arriving to the compound at the end of September when I first arrived in Syria, I sat in the passenger seat of the lead truck while the ODA 21 team sergeant, Justin, drove me around. I didn't know at the time that I was about to learn what true battlefield love was. The team sergeant was one of the best noncommissioned officers whom I had ever had the opportunity to work alongside, the kind of individual with whom I would stand shoulder to shoulder in any fight. His personality and demeanor exhibit leadership, and he demanded perfection from not only himself but also his soldiers and those around him. In his presence, I heard Forrest Gump's voice in my head: *I hope I don't let him down.*

After a self-guided tour of the compound, I found the room where I would spend just about all my free time, the kitchen. Right next to the kitchen was where I would find love in a very *Flintstones* kind of way. Beyond the door to the stairs that led up to the main floor where we lived was a kennel. At the time, there were two puppies there, affectionately known as Bacon and Meatloaf. These two Syrian trash dogs quickly became the center of our attention. Now that was battlefield love. The owner of the dog attempted to train the dogs before they were shipped to Iraq to be transported to the United States. There is an amazing nongovernmental organization called the SPCAI that ships animals that military personnel fall in love with to the States at little cost to the servicemember.

Two months later, and now November, I was running the perimeter of the compound that I had run many times with my new friend Joe, the leader of the SF team. Enjoying the sun on my face while listening to an audiobook and trying to catch my breath after a run, I heard an awful sound overpowering the voice in my ears. The sound was that of something being tortured. The hair on the back of my neck stood up, sending chills down my spine. I had nothing besides my knife to protect myself with, but knowing my own lethality with a knife, I shrugged and turned toward the sound. I picked up the pace, trotting straight toward the sound, hoping that I could help prevent whatever evil was happening. As I got closer, the noise grew louder and became a shriek that almost made me sick to my stomach and sent my mind to wondering what was occurring.

I debated if I should return to the operation center or not, but ultimately I decided that doing so would take up too much time, and right now time was too precious of a commodity. Rounding a corner of the building, I was immediately struck by what was happening. One of our partner Syrian soldiers had a litter of puppies at his feet. The screaming was coming from them. At first sight, I thought they were shrieking in pain for some reason. Noticing that their fur was covered in a matte red color, I approached the Syrian, smoothly fingering the knife that I kept in my appendix carry position. "Hey! Excuse me. What is going on?!" is what I tried to say in an authoritative voice in Arabic. The Syrian whipped around with a shirt that will forever remain stained red. I saw him staring at the long knife he was gingerly holding in his right hand. He held a puppy in his left hand.

Getting a closer look at the situation, I saw that he was cutting the ears and tails off the dogs. I remembered that the Syrian shepherds use these dogs, a breed known as Anatolian shepherds, to protect their sheep from bears. The weakest spots on the dogs are their ears and tails. When a bear grabs the dog's tail or ears, the dog submits to the bear and dies, so the shepherds cut the ears and tails off when the puppies are only a few days old. I had to stop it even though it was a local custom. "You know who I am," I said, looking him in the eyes but keeping an eye on his right hand. "Please stop doing this." He shook his head back and forth, telling me that he would not stop, which meant we were going to have a problem.

"The only way you can stop me is if you buy one of the unharmed dogs." Looking at him, I knew that there were many other possibilities. Killing him would have made me feel better, but then what? We would have had to leave the region, and our relationship with our partner force would have been shot. As the guy who held the relationships, I concluded that this would not go over well. So, not many options. I nodded in reply.

While watching the man, I bent over, picked up the only dog that had been left unharmed, and stuffed it in my shirt. "I will provide payment to Ageed [the local Syrian commander] tonight for you at our nightly sync meeting." He nodded. I swiftly made my exit, heading for the door to our compound.

I headed up to the operation center and informed the team commander that we had another dog. He asked me to have the dog checked out by the medics and asked what its name was. At that moment, Ghadir walked into the room and announced that she had made dinner with the other linguists. We were going to be eating lamb chops with rice and corn. Nodding, I made that that Syrian dog's name: Lambchop.

I called home to tell Sam about the puppy, but I didn't go into too much detail. She begged me to find someone else to keep him because, at the time, we had two dogs, two rabbits, four ducks, and ten chickens already at home. It was hard enough already for her to take care of so many heartbeats. I knew she wouldn't mind just one more, but I figured something out. Ghadir decided to adopt Lambchop as her puppy. This quickly became a point of friction between us, but the tension quickly lifted and I thanked her for taking care of him.

One day we had an important visitor to our compound, so we had to tactically hide the animals. We put Lamby in a back room with bacon and meat loaf and sat back there listening to music. Before we knew it, there was a very intimidating presence standing in the doorway. "How are you doing?" General Votel commented with a smirk on his face. It was not every day that we were graced with the man in charge of the entire war, so I was a bit taken aback, but not Ghadir. She was General Votel's personal linguist when he came to the area. With the puppies playing around us, he stepped into the room and scratched Lamby behind his ears, at which point I let out a deep breath that I didn't realize I was holding. He chatted with Ghadir for a little bit while playing with the dogs, and then he was gone.

A few weeks later, I coordinated shipment of the dogs from our compound, across Syria and Iraq, and to my team's compound back in Iraq. This was the same team I originally had deployed with. I contacted Chief Michael, who was just as excited as I was to have puppies living in his room. I am pretty sure he cleaned off my old bed just for Lamby. The driver met up with the organization that ensured the dogs had their shots and flew them to the United States. Once in the United States, they were transported home. Lamby went to service dog training through the SPCAI. For anyone wondering how Samantha handled this, I'll say that once she met Lambchop, it was love at first sight. She adores him and spoils him *rotten*!

SPCAI, I thank you for helping with our puppies. To everyone who helped bring Lambchop home to us, we thank you very much!

12

Chief Jon

Iron sharpens iron, and one man sharpens another.

—Proverbs 27:17

Why in my mind do I picture him always smiling? This is something that I have mulled over in my head. I feel that the answer lies in the interactions I had with him. Shortly after he arrived in Syria in December, I met him, a guy who stood out more than anyone else. Besides the fact he was easily a foot and a half taller than I, he just had the type of personality that made everyone enjoy being around him. His name was Jon, like mine, so I knew I would not forget it. Jon was introduced to me as my new Special Forces army chief warrant officer. His green beret stood out, and I knew he would be a great addition to our team. Thank goodness he was so large, because he had big shoes to fill, replacing my best friend, Chief Mike, who was still in Iraq and who I wished were here in Syria with me. Jon's arrival completed Team Manbij's roster. I quickly found that working alongside him made the job I had in Syria one of the most enjoyable times I had ever had on a deployment. In the very short amount of time that he was with us, I found that he was someone whom I could talk to about anything. He was the type of guy who was very charismatic and always wanted people to be happy. He put his family first always, and I knew he loved God by the way he treated everyone he met. It was encouraging to be around him.

"I hate ISIS!" Chief said during one of our team brainstorming sessions. This was not something that I had expected to hear out of him. Chief Jon was always the definition of professional, so an outburst like this grabbed our attention. This very moment, we were observing the local customs, drinking Turkish coffee, and smoking a hookah. This was our opportunity to unwind after a long day. Everyone joined us on the compound at least once, including friends from other US bases in the area. Chief was standing while holding a cup of coffee in his left hand that had come from the TOC freshly prepared. This had become a common tradition for a few of us and was one of the most fun things that we did as a team. We originally met in a back corner of the building, where we kept ourselves secluded from the sleeping quarters because we were prone to getting loud. Once our coalition friends moved in and occupied our secret hookah lounge by force, we relocated to one of the battle positions that we intended to make into a kitchen later. Ghadir never forgave the French for stealing our serenity spot. She would often ask if I wanted to prank the French, which is something I would fall prey to. If the French ever found out it was I who boarded up their door, I apologize, but it was funny listening to their story of rappelling down to the first floor and walking around the building just to use the bathroom and never clearing their door, but instead using a ladder to get back into their room. Of course, we removed the obstruction when they offered to cook dinner, because their crepes were pretty tasty, and we got to quote Ricky Bobby from the movie *Talladega Nights* throughout the whole dinner. After one such dinner, we were forced to show them the movie, after which they started acting like the Frenchman, which got weird. But it was funny.

"I am getting sick of the IEDs along the road between us and the tower base," Chief said, continuing his discussion from earlier. The tower base was home to our US counterpart force led by Lieutenant Colonel Matt and his Third Calvary Regiment infantry scouts. They were some amazing soldiers. I wasn't the only one who took every opportunity to travel the couple of miles to their base. I enjoyed their company, and their dining facility usually had a surprisingly good assortment of delicious hot food. Again, I must be careful what I admit to, but I will say that it wasn't too long after this that we started attending a weekly sync meeting with the Third Calvary Regiment leadership and they noticed their pies were disappearing from the refrigerator in their dining facility. When they came to our compound and ate dinner with us, they noticed the dessert we provided them as being something that had originated from their base. It was a great relationship: we traded information for food—my kind of business. Because of the high amount of predictable travel between our bases, ISIS increased IED attacks along the route traveled, with the IEDs hitting our partner forces more times than they hit US forces. Spitballing solutions was almost always effective, and today I felt that it was going to be one of those days. Chief continued, "So, what do we do? I am not going to stop going there, and I don't want to take another way just to get dinner." This brought out a chorus of laughter from those of us sitting in a circle around the hookahs.

The smoking session lasted the typical two hours. We jumped from topic to topic, until one person ruined the fun by standing up and calling it a night. After the first person leaves, everyone leaves. The last two in the lounge were usually me and either Chief or Ghadir. I was the person to stand first this time, though. I wanted to call my wife and see how my son was doing. After standing, I asked Ghadir to walk with me, which she did. Walking back to my room with Ghadir on my left, I slowed my roll to chat. "Can you contact our guy in the government and the military and see if we can talk to him in person tomorrow at lunch here?" She just nodded her head.

The next day as we all sat down around a large wooden table, Ghadir translated for the commander of the Manbij Military

Council and the civil administrator of Manbij. Chief spoke, saying, "We see a big problem is the number of IED attacks along the main road here." Our visitors nodded as he spoke.

The military commander interrupted Chief, stating, "We have patrols on that road constantly, but ISIS still places IEDs under our noses. It is the deadliest area for us in our region."

Once he was finished, I piped up: "Sir, what do you think is a solution to this?" Surprise that I had spoken was written on everyone's face. I might have been the team leader, but I didn't have the authority of Chief. The commander shook his head back and forth while shrugging his shoulders. I almost chuckled to myself, murmuring, "I understood that Arabic." Looking our visitors in the eyes, I presented them with a solution: "I learned over the past few years that distance is a great equalizer. I am a good shot, but as the distance increases between my target and my rifle, I have a much harder time of hitting it. Do you think theory would hold true for an IED?" Seeing them nod their heads, I knew I had buy-in for what I was about to propose.

"If we increased the road from two lanes to four lanes, then ISIS couldn't place IEDs close enough to hurt us effectively. It would also provide jobs to the city administration, thus providing further legitimacy while protecting the people." I liked what I saw on their faces. They were fully committed to the proposal.

After Chief presented a well-thought-out plan, our visitors returned to their respective locations. Jon walked up to me, and rather than giving me a simple high five or a handshake, he embraced me in one of his infamous bear hugs. "Jon, *we did it!*" I smiled from ear to ear, but I also knew I would have to help the civil administration allocate funds to pay for the operation.

Ghadir, Chief, and I would spend no fewer than three days a week at the government building helping to put everything in place for this operation. Within a month, the road was wider and IEDs were eliminated, thus further restricting ISIS's ability to inflict fear into the population by publicly targeting the government and coalition by placing IEDs along a major service road. Most importantly, we could travel to get our pies without a high likelihood of an IED strike. Team Manbij (minus) won again thanks to Chief's brilliance and his ability to think outside the box. I love you, brother.

To Chief's Family

This is one look into the human who was not only my friend but also, an even higher honor, my teammate while in Syria.

There was not much to do on our compound in Manbij, so we spent a lot of time together talking or watching movies and TV. Deep physiological discussions helped pass the time while we were not going out into sector. One such discussion with Chief. Chief had his chair leaned back in the tactical operations center, and it was just him and me alone in the room. We were talking religion. He surprised me with an observation: "Jon." He was always very formal when in the presence of anyone, but when we were alone, I begged him to address me by my first name, as a friend. "I am not scared to die. You see, as of right now I have a perfect wife and four amazing children. I cannot protect them no matter how awesome you think I am, but I tell you what, my friend, if I die with honor in service to our great country, I will go to heaven because I am a Christian. Up in that amazing place I will be able not only to protect my entire family all the time but also to do it and not get tired."

I will give you the keys of the kingdom of heaven, and whatever you bind on earth shall be bound in heaven, and whatever you lose on earth shall be loose in heaven.

—Matthew 16:19

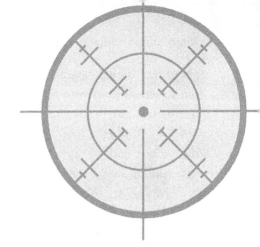

13

Brigadier General Pond

He lifted me out of the slimy pit, out of the mud and mire;
he set my feet on a rock and gave me a firm place to stand.

—Psalm 40:2

Leadership is about far more than I ever learned at West Point.

As a coalition, we entertained people of many different nationalities in our sector. I was often chosen for the mission as a touch point for the people since I was the civil affairs officer for the team and I had a unique perspective on the area, including a focus on, and an awareness of, the people. One day I found myself in the lead vehicle of a convoy escorting one of the leaders of the British military in Syria around Manbij. We often took high-ranking individuals to the government building, a school such as Ramadan Hiju (the former ISIS headquarters), serving as the military headquarters. Today I had something special planned.

"Chief, turn right onto the service road up here." I pointed with my hand while looking at him to make sure he understood.

"Sir, do you want me to go to the shawarma place?" Chief asked. It was a good logical question. My stomach grumbled as I thought about it. I thought perhaps we could make a small adjustment to our itinerary, no matter how much trouble I would get in later for having done so.

"No, brother. I need to take the general to the hospital." With that, Chief nodded and took the service road that led right to the gate leading into the hospital. I keyed the mic on my radio. "This is convoy leader. We are making a short stop at the hospital. Only essential personnel are needed inside the hospital. Convoy leader out." We circled the vehicles in front of the three-story building. I stepped out of my truck. Dr. Reem, the hospital administrator, practically ran out of the hospital's front door and greeted me with a huge smile and a hug. I turned her attention to the tall man quickly walking up to us. "Dr. Reem, I have the humble privilege of introducing you to Brigadier General Pond." Brigadier General Pond extended his hand, and Dr. Reem shook it, greeting him and welcoming him to Furat Hospital.

I escorted the English officer around the hospital for about an hour, explaining the shortcomings and what my plans were to bridge the gaps. Walking into the surgery room, we saw a sight that will stay with me as long as I live. A surgeon was sitting against a wall with his face in his hands, hunched over and appearing to be sobbing. There was blood on the floor, and the operating table was a mess with tools all over the place and the room covered in organic tissue. Quickly diverting my vision from the room, I turned to Reem. "What happened?" She grabbed my hand and led me across the hallway to the secondary operating room, which was void of any equipment.

"Jon, you know that we are trying to get equipment for this room. Today we had a soldier who was wounded in an explosion. He was brought here immediately, but the surgeon was working on someone else. And since this room isn't capable of receiving any patients, the soldier had to wait. By the time he was able to be worked on, it was too late. I believe if the soldier had been worked on immediately when he was brought in, he would have survived, and his family would not be downstairs grieving at the moment." Reem had tears running down her face, so I opened my arms and gave her a solid hug.

"I will fix this, Reem. Thank you for telling me this." I knew it was critical to our military mission, the local government, and the people that we found a way forward to renovating the hospital. Reem told me that the previous Civil Affairs Team worked on starting the project to renew the surgical room. I knew that if we successfully completed the project, the military, local government, and civilian population, would benefit. I prayed that I could fix the hospital and ifwe increased the hospitals surgical capability that we would never need to use the surgical room. It felt good to know that no matter what, there was a medical capability started by my predicessors and would be available for coalition Forces when we started up offensive operations against ISIS in the region. . I never once thought that I understood what a small change to the medical infrastructure, namely, the hospital, would have on the overall importance of needing an open hospital room at all times, but would soon find out why. The brigadier general, clearing his throat behind me, broke up the moment. I turned from the empty surgery room and followed him down the hallway. Walking down the stairs, I explained what Reem had told me.

As we reached the main floor and turned toward Dr. Reem's offices, Brigadier General Pond turned to me and issued an order: "Captain Turnbull, get me some paper and a pen, please."

"Yes, sir." I turned to one of my contacts in the hospital named Mona and asked her for the stationery, which she provided promptly. Much to my amazement, Brigadier General Pond sat down and began writing a note to the family of the deceased soldier. After he had finished it, he passed it to Ghadir, who translated it and then handed it to Dr. Reem. Dr. Reem continued to cry as she received the note.

That may have been the most amazing display of leadership I have ever witnessed in my entire life. No matter how bad life may be, there are people out there in the world like Brigadier General Pond who will go out of their way to write a nice note of encouragement to pull someone out of the rut they find themselves in. Once Brigadier General Pond had returned to the coalition headquarters, he told his staff about what happened. Someone from Pond's staff called me and told me to get a quote for fixing the second room with the equipment needed, which I did. The British military funded the project. I would later be treated in that very room for wounds sustained from an explosion. The equipment that had been provided by Brigadier General Pond's office would be what kept me alive.

Brigadier General Pond, one day when I grow up, I will be like you. God bless you in your endeavors.

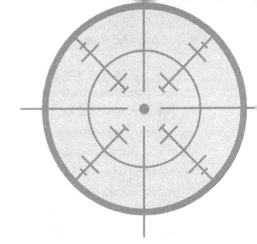

14

Manbij Half-Marathon Turkey Trot

> Do you know that in a race all the runners run, but only one gets the prize? Run in such a way as to get the prize.
>
> —1 Corinthians 9:24

When I first arrived in Syria, after showing me to my accommodations, where I dropped my bag off on my cot, Justin, the SF team sergeant, introduced me to his Special Forces team alongside of whom I would be working. I was excited to get to work with this team. My heart raced as Justin introduced me as their "special friend" who would be living with them. He made sure that the team understood who I was and that they were to help me out if I needed any assistance. To my amazement, by the time he was finished speaking, I was an honorary member of ODA 21 (with ODA standing for Operational Detachments–A). Again, I heard Forrest Gump's voice in my head: *I hope I don't let him down.* The team then conducted a routine shift changeover briefing that highlighted the activities of the day, making sure that everyone knew what had occurred and what was going to occur over the next twenty-four hours. This single event demonstrated the effectiveness and professionalism of ODA 21.

For the last half of their deployment, which was to end in December, there was almost no mass confusion as is common in the fog of war. This is because the communication among this team was very strong and open. One topic caught my interest as Joe, the team leader, started speaking. The group proposed a team-building event for when they returned to Fort Campbell, Kentucky, where their unit was based. They wanted to conduct an ultramarathon together. Hearing this, I smirked as I mumbled, "Misery loves company." Everyone around me chuckled. My comment got me in hot water though. I turned red as Joe singled me out.

"Welcome to the club, Jon. We are practicing for the race and would like to have you join us. On Thanksgiving Day, we are doing a half-marathon here. Will you join us?"

Really?! He had a smile forming on his face because he knew that he had me. I nodded. In an attempt at humor to dig myself out of the hole I had dug, I stated, "Of course, brother. I will even supply the turkey meal for lunch afterward, along with the General Order Number 1 Exception to Policy: Liquid." The GO1 Exemption to Policy referred to alcohol in combat; only a few units were permitted to drink alcohol. I needed to think before speaking. Everyone in the room cheered for booze, but Joe and Justin shook their heads no. "Okay, just the turkey and the run then," I spoke.

The next morning, Joe woke me around six o'clock. Walking down the cement stairs with him, still clearing the sleep from my eyes, I commented, "If this is a warning of how things are going to be, I am going to have to lock and bar my door."

"You don't have to run. You asked me to wake you up," Joe said with a skip in his step. Stepping outside, I found that the sun was shining bright, already giving off its heat. We walked around the outdoor shower trailer and cut between it and the kitchen trailer, which already had a wonderful aroma coming from it. "When we finish running, we will have to see what Ghadir cooked for breakfast," Joe said with a smile on his face. This is something that I would learn quickly and would awake early most days for. Ghadir was by far the best cook on the compound. She loved to cook, and found any opportunity she could to do so. I recall her mentioning that she was not the chef, but she would cook large portions every time she prepared herself something in case anyone else was hungry. We made sure that no one took advantage of her hospitality and that everyone appreciated everything she did without making degrading comments. Instead, they would give her their thanks.

Joe and I walked a little way for a warm-up and opened one of our sliding security gates before we took off at a trot. I turned my Garmin watch on to see the distance. We ran along the perimeter road. Circling the compound, it ran along the outer security wall. This was my first glimpse of the compound. I was amazed by it. The team called it the Tay-Tay—for Taylor Swift—Memorial Grain Silos for good reason. Standing tall in the face of nothing were eight huge cement grain silos. As we ran around them, Joe told me why my nose had curled at the smell. "Jon, that smell isn't me. When the coalition took this place from ISIS, their final stronghold was on top of the grain silos. Inside the TOC, there is a picture of the exact moment when the coalition dropped huge bombs on top of the silos, killing the final ISIS fighters. When the SDF went up to remove the bodies, they dumped them into the silos, where they remain to this day. Therefore, that smell is a combination of rotting grain and ISIS filth." The odor cut me to the core; I would smell it anywhere on our compound. The worst was while showering. I know that the first rule of showering is never to fart in the shower, but I have now added to that, "Don't build a shower where there is a rotting corpse nearby."

We ran around the silos, and then the compound opened into a big field. At each end of the open area was a large white box that marked the area as a soccer field. We continued our run around the field and then had to pass through another security gate. This one was manned by one of the soldiers from our partner force. He opened the gate for us after we stopped, and Joe talked to him for a few seconds. Joe told me that there was no code but that the guards would open the gate for me anytime they saw me running. After jogging around the back side of our compound, he and I were back to where we had started, and there were two more team guys there getting ready to run. I looked down at my watch and was disappointed to see that the route around the compound was a distance of 0.48 miles. This would make any distance running difficult and would mess with previous my times.

We ran a few miles. Joe introduced me to the stairs that were accessible at the back of our compound for, as Joe put it, when I needed a good workout. There were about ten flights of stairs. By the time we had run up and down a couple of times, I submitted to his dominance, using breakfast as my excuse. I was not disappointed by Ghadir's breakfast of scrambled eggs, flatbread, and a meat that I might have been a little too scared to ask what it was.

So, time went by, and before I knew it Thanksgiving was upon us. Waking early became a common occurrence. We had just about everyone outside the kitchen, assembled to run the first ever Manbij Half-Marathon Turkey Trot. There was no gunshot to start the race—for good reason—but it was a bad course. On this day, I was at the height of my physical performance. Since the track wasn't a full half mile, we had to run an odd number of times around our compound. I hit the distance around thirty-three laps and sat down next to the kitchen to breathe in the delicious aromas while waiting for my friends to complete their laps. I fished out a few bottles of water from the fridge while saying hello to Chief, Kyle, and Ghadir, who were preparing our Thanksgiving dinner, the food for which Ghadir had helped me procure from a local farmer. We didn't have anything as grand as a deep fryer for the turkey, so Ghadir cooked one in the oven. Kyle cooked some breasts on our grill, and then our psyops guys tried to boil a turkey as if in a deep fryer. Don't do that. Deep-fried meat is different from boiled.

As we celebrated everything we were thankful for at dinner, I had the privilege of presenting my new team and family with one more surprise. I walked into our dining room holding a large serving tray with a couple of pumpkin pies on it. Steam was still rising from them. It was an aroma that made me think of home and of my grandma's cooking. I may have passed the pies off as having baked them myself, until someone said they had seen them in the fridge at the Third Calvary Regiment base. Then everyone laughed at me, throwing rolls and anything else they could find. It was a great evening, a night I will remember for my entire life—an amazing day starting off with a physical challenge and finishing with gluttony.

15

Post–Turkey Day

In everything I did, I showed you that by this kind of hard work we must help the weak, remembering the words the Lord Jesus himself said: "It is more blessed to give than receive."

—Acts 20:35

I slept like a baby after working out and eating so much turkey. Upon awaking, my legs felt more like Jell-O than anything useful, but I got them to work to carry me down to the bathroom. On my return up the stairs to my room, my roommate Brian was walking down the stairs and grabbed me. We walked out to the kitchen to make breakfast. My stomach was growling, and I was looking forward to a turkey omelet. This is a tradition that Samantha and I have had since our first Thanksgiving together in 2006. Walking out into the sunlight, I discovered that the stench in the air was far worse than normal. I had been prepared for the acidic odor, but this cut way more to the core than any odor at any other time. Looking around quickly, I saw there was a lot of liquid surrounding the shower trailer and backup generators. "Do you smell that?" Brian asked.

"It wasn't me," I grunted while nodding, lifting my shirt to cover my nose. "There must be a septic backup. Can you make breakfast? I will make a quick phone call about this before the team wakes up and we have to leave from this location because of poor sanitation." We went our separate ways, he continuing to the kitchen and I turning back into the building. I ran up the flight of stairs and went straight to Ghadir's room. I knocked lightly, not wanting to wake our PAO (public affairs officer) and suffer her wrath, and then poked my head in after hearing Ghadir telling me to enter.

Sitting at the end of her bed, on a lockbox, I avoided the rug she had down so I wouldn't track anything into her room. I began telling her why I smelled bad. She jumped out of bed and grabbed her phone before following me to the meeting room across the hallway. We sat down at the table and made a quick phone call to the Civil Administration of Manbij (CAM), the local government whose rule of law I had to enhance in the eyes of the people. Ghadir secured a time slot with the sanitation department to come out and clean our sewer system. While working, we attracted a small crowd. Everyone laughed when they heard what was going on. We blamed the boiled turkey for the backup. After a short time, a sanitation truck arrived and cleaned out the system. Once that job was finished, a gentleman in a suit walked up to our front fence and asked for an audience with me. Our Syrian Democratic Forces (SDF) counterparts escorted him to our meeting room and gave him refreshments before I arrived.

When I sat down, the man introduced himself as the chairman of the Sanitation Division of the CAM and said that he had a problem he thought I could help him with as I had helped the medical and education committees. "Seven years ago, when ISIS took control of Manbij, they neglected the sewer system. Over the last seven years, the system has become clogged much like your system here, but the people cannot get it fixed like you Americans. As a result, every year many people die from diseases due to the filth. I propose that thirty men be hired to work under me for one month to clean out the worst parts of the city. This would cost no more than fifteen thousand dollars. Can you help the people of Manbij, Captain Turnbull?"

I scratched my beard and stood to shake his hand. I thanked him in Arabic and told him that I would talk to my team and do what I could. In my head, I saw this as an operation right up my alley: little risk, low cost, high return on my investment, and an opportunity to delegitimize ISIS without our having to do any of the heavy lifting. After the man left, I sat down with my team to have a brainstorming session.

"Let me lay it out for everyone as I see it. Pros: Little cost. All funds go to the local economy. It makes the CAM look good, which will aid in legitimizing the local government. It delegitimizes ISIS further, gives us further access to and influence in the area, and prevents us from having to retrograde from here because of poor sanitation. Cons: I don't have OpFund at this time, but I can always find money." I finished by sitting down and trying to listen to as many little conversations that popped up between individuals as I could. That evening I decided that this was something we would do. There were no objections, so I opened my personal computer and, using my email application, sent a request for funds to the Spirit of America organization, which had helped me on numerous occasions. Continuing the nonprofit's reputation for providing a quick response, Spirit of America approved the project the next day. Then we started working on how to move the funds from the United States to our location. At the end of the day, one of my linguists, named Ubed, picked up a wire transfer while he was passing through Erbil, with the aid of my teammates there, then brought the funds to us in Syria.

The day after he arrived, I was sitting in the office of the sanitation administrator. There was a small table between him and me, and I was laying out stacks of hundred-dollar bills. He signed a piece of paper stating he had received the money from me. The man put his office staff to work immediately. Another job done by Team Manbij that allowed us to stay in the area to continue fighting against ISIS while legitimizing the local government by having the people see that their sanitation system was drastically improved by Syrians working in the sewers with buckets for removal of the waste.

16

Shannon Kent's Scarves

> Do not let your adorning be external—the braiding of
> hair and the putting on gold jewelry, or the clothing you
> wear—but let your adorning be the hidden person of
> the heart with the imperishable beauty of a gentle and
> quiet spirit, which in God's sight is very precious.
>
> —1 Peter 3:3–4

A few days after Thanksgiving, while enjoying a cup of coffee and looking through previous mission briefings, I saw an email from a naval chief named Shannon Kent that outlined the importance of our area of operations and the important strategic opportunities that were available. I copied her email and sent a short email of introduction, asking if she would like to reengage the mission in my area. She responded almost immediately, saying that she was on her way to our location. She had worked with the previous team, but there was little to no continuity or carryover from them to me.

When she arrived, she sat down with Ghadir, and the two of them talked over possibilities and opportunities in Manbij. One of the team grabbed me from the TOC and took me to join the duo.

Ghadir told Shannon that I had the best understanding of and relationships with the government officials and many other residents and civilians inside Manbij. If Shannon wanted to expand her information network, she should talk to me, Ghadir said. Shannon and I talked in-depth about what she was trying to accomplish. She told me her senior's objectives and how I could facilitate.

We came up with a good plan of action. After a few emails back and forth, Shannon was standing in our operations center. We discussed the projects that we would be involved in and what she wanted to accomplish in my area of operations. I reminded her that I owned most of the civilian relationships within the city and would be more than happy to share them with her. As a team, we walked downstairs to our motor pool, where our vehicles were safeguarded, and mounted up. After I had communication with my higher headquarters, we drove downtown, parking near the local bazaar.

We left a few of our guys behind with the vehicles as security, along with a couple of Syrian soldiers, and then walked into the bazaar. The bazaar in Manbij was what back home in the States we would consider a farmers market. People would sell items such as fruit, vegetables, and clothing. Shannon took a different route to meet with a contact, and Ghadir and I walked around the bazaar looking for a few gifts to mail back home, as Christmas was approaching. We exchanged our US dollars for Syrian pounds at a shop in the bazaar, and on this particular day we purchased a bathrobe called a *farawa*. After buying the local garment, we continued to walk around the shops. Ghadir had a lot of children walking up to her and wanting to give her hugs. Many of the same children would walk up to me and call me by my rank and last name and then give me a high five, thanking me for protecting them. Walking around carrying a rifle on my back, I was pretty sure they believed that with me there, they were safe.

I'm going to backtrack a bit here, so bear with me. In 2015, my best friend was deployed to Turkey. He recommended destroying an ISIS training camp that used to be a college in Manbij. After the recommendation had made its way through the appropriate channels, the training camp was no more. The bombing was historical for many reasons, but given the classification level of this story, let me just state that the building was destroyed. Bearing in mind the significance of this event, I walked around the destroyed building one day with Ghadir and mentioned that I wanted to take a piece of the rubble back for my friend. She grabbed a few pieces of rebar from it so I could present them to my buddy as a memento of his actions. Later, Ghadir approached me, looking worried, which was rare because she is the strongest woman I have ever met. "Jon, I am scared. I don't feel safe sometimes when we are out on a mission. I know that I cannot carry a handgun, so that thought is out of the question. You have been working out with me, and at times we practice fighting with our hands. You are also teaching me how to fight with a knife. I have an idea of something we can do to help me. It'll also give you something really cool to give your friend who dropped the bomb on the ISIS training facility."

This rattled me because it was my job to protect Ghadir. If she didn't feel safe, then I had failed her. Since it was illegal for her to carry a pistol all the time, I got to work on training her in some basic hand-to-hand combat. I knew how to work the pointy end of a knife and started working with her on self-defense using a knife.

Back to the bazaar: We had about three hours to kill while Shannon was on her mission, and Ghadir had the perfect idea for what to do. She led me to a part of the bazaar where there was loud banging. Hearing it before we were even close, I knew it was a blacksmith shop. Turning a corner, I was excited to see an older gentleman training two youths to mold metal to a purpose. I have done a lot of blacksmithing in my life, so I felt a kindred spirit to these men. Seeing me in his workplace, the blacksmith approached me and Ghadir. Ghadir started talking to him. He nodded again and again. She surprised me by pulling the pieces of rebar out of her purse and handing them to him. While standing there, he stuffed them into his furnace and soon pulled them back out, holding the hot orange end with forceps. Then he instructed the young men on where to hit and when.

The blacksmiths created three knives out of the rebar in about thirty minutes. I paid the gentlemen for their services, and Ghadir and I started back to the vehicles. Almost back to the trucks, Shannon appeared from out of nowhere. She eyed me up and down, laughing at my leather bathrobe, and nodded in approval. Just before we reached the trucks, I halted our movement at one of my most favorite places in all of Manbij. I spent about ten dollars buying a local dish called man'ousheh. These little treats were like small pizzas or sweets. I had to make sure we had enough for everyone who had stayed behind to protect our vehicles. We bought plenty, except I hadn't considered how many Shannon could eat. A block later, when we arrived at the trucks, the snacks were devoured. Shannon felt bad that there were none for our security team, so she went back to the dealer and bought a bunch more for our guards.

That is what I remember about Shannon, not that she could eat a lot of delicious food, but that she had a huge heart and would go the extra mile to help anyone. She didn't need a linguist because she spoke more languages than I can pronounce or think of off the top of my head. Shannon lived on a separate compound from ours, so we didn't get to know her as we would have liked. But we did appreciate everything she did for us. Not only was she a hard worker who got her jobs done quickly, but also she happened to live next to a store that sold a commodity that we couldn't get in our town. Alcohol could not be found anywhere in Manbij, so we asked her for some every time she came to our base. She wouldn't allow us to give her any money for it, but seeing as she loved scarves, we would trade scarves for this precious commodity. Thanks to Shannon, we had champagne to ring in the New Year, along with a few other items to celebrate with, and we'd have some for Ghadir's upcoming birthday. To Shannon's husband Joe, I want to apologize for the number of scarves that were sent home. Please know that they mean a great deal to everyone we worked with.

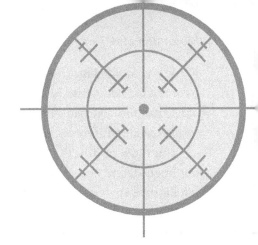

17

Scott Wirtz and Our First Mission

A friend loves at all times, and a brother
is born for a time of adversity.

—Proverbs 17:17

In mid-December, early in the morning, Shannon got out of her truck and motioned for everyone in her truck, as well as those in the second truck, to get out. This was going to be the first meeting of every member of Cross-Functional Team Manbij. A shorter, well-built man, with his hands and arms covered in tattoos, got out of the passenger's side of the second truck and walked up to me with Shannon. He held his hand out as Shannon introduced him as Petty Officer Second Class (PO2) Scott Wirtz. I must have had a confused look on my face because Shannon said, "Petty officer is a similar rank to a sergeant in the army."

Scotty grasped my hand and said, "You can call me Sergeant Scotty if that makes you more comfortable, sir."

I nodded, saying, "It is a pleasure to meet you, Scotty. I would like it if you called me Jon in most situations. My dad was a sir, and I am not old enough to be a sir yet. Plus, you look at least ten years older than me." He had a firm handshake. With a smirk on his face, he looked me in the eyes, telling me it was a pleasure.

I introduced him to Chief Jon, our operations officer; Ghadir, our linguist; and two sergeants named Joe and Devin who were our intelligence analysts. Devin was a young guy with a good head on his shoulders. He was one of the only guys whose sense of humor was similar to mine, and he reminded me of my brother-in-law, Steven. No wonder we got along so well. I looked forward to any opportunity I had to work alongside him. We would sit and chat quite a bit throughout the workdays since our desks were next to each other.

My team loaded our equipment and personnel into their two vehicles. I checked radios and called up to my higher headquarters to say "Game on" as we prepared to drive through the gate. I jumped in the driver's seat of the second vehicle, which became the lead vehicle for the convoy. Shannon protested my leading the convoy, obviously thinking that because most convoy commanders would be toward the back of the line of vehicles, I should do the same. But since I was assuming command of the team and I knew where we were going, I won the proverbial coin toss. Scotty argued that I shouldn't be the driver, but I won the argument by saying that even though I was higher in rank, he was more experienced, and I valued his experience over my rank. I needed him as the truck commander (TC), I told him. He nodded in approval!

When I took command of my first civil affairs team (CAT) in 2015, after the qualification course I learned that my team sergeant, Sergeant First Class Timmy B, had wrested control of our team from a lower-ranking soldier during a minor altercation. Our soldier had tried to fight him, and he, my team sergeant, punched him in the throat. That throat punch became a thing of legend. I didn't need a throat punch; I acknowledged experience and somehow had earned my team's respect without one. The fact that Team Manbij honored me as their team commander or team leader is the greatest honor that I have ever been given and probably ever will be given.

While I was driving the truck into the heart of Manbij, Scotty asked me who I was and where I was from. We started talking about guns, and he got excited to hear that I was a triggerman and that I spent many hours of my life behind a rifle. Being our team's token Navy SEAL, he was the team's triggerman. He said that he was nervous about the fact that he was the only person who would have to fight if it came down to it, but since I was a fighter, he said, he could relax just a bit with the knowledge that I would watch his back if he asked. We would spend many hours talking about shooting together and going hunting together upon our return to the States. I promised him that I would take him deer hunting in northern Michigan with my family and then try getting us on a large game hunt in Montana, as well as take him out on the best deep-sea fishing charter operated by the best sea captain in North Carolina whom I know personally, a guy named Von. I told Scotty that not only had Captain Von helped me catch big fish, but also the experience was a great destresser and therapy for PTSD. Scotty agreed, nodding his head to the prospect of getting out on the water, which he let me know was his natural environment. He then shocked me by saying that after we caught a couple of huge fish a few miles offshore, he would race my team back to the beach, us in the boat and him swimming the couple of miles. He asked me if I would participate in shooting competitions with him, which was something I had never considered before this moment.

What I respected most about Scotty was that he was reliable and had the qualities I needed in a teammate. Scotty called me "Sir" until I ordered him to call me "Jon," which he did with much hesitation. I told him that I needed a friend on the team more than a subordinate. He was far more experienced than I, and I wanted his opinion as a friend rather than as an obedient subordinate. During mission briefings I would always pull Scotty aside, away from the team, and ask him bluntly, "Scotty, speak to me. What is wrong with my plan, and how do we make it better?" He always gave me blunt feedback, and I valued his expertise. When Scotty spoke, I shut my mouth and internalized what was said. Most every time we did what he had recommended. Everyone on Team Manbij knew that Captain Jonno was the team commander, but everyone also knew that Scotty was really in charge of ground operations. I oversaw the operations. Scotty was in charge of the tactics and the fighting. Little did I know at the time of meeting Scotty Wirtz that he would one day mean more to me than just being a friend.

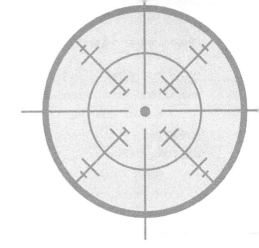

18

"Okay, Scotty, Let's Do Some Good!"

In the cover of your presence you hide them from the plots of men, you store them in your shelter from the strife of tongues.

—Psalm 31:20

The use of nonlethal aid is another way to accomplish a military objective. I continue to amaze myself at how effective I am at accomplishing my higher command's objectives while alleviating suffering, the latter of which is the mission of USAID, not the military. After the sanitation operation, I drove by the hospital to a large reservoir where the government was digging out what ISIS had neglected. The government wanted to show me where the sanitation would flow from the city. And then when it rained, the sewage would flow out into the countryside and fertilize the farmland. I made sure to remind myself not to eat any of the produce ever again. The reservoir was a large expanse. While we stood watching large Syrian Democratic Forces tractors digging at the ground, showing a great working relationship between the military and the local government, a local shop owner brought us some local tea and a few plastic chairs.

The shop owner was a travel coordinator, and she wanted to talk about the world. Having never been anywhere outside of Manbij, she asked us about the United States and other places we had been. I was made uncomfortable by her questions, so I started asking questions of my own. At some point I asked her about the area and if there were any ISIS fighters around, expecting a quick no. To my amazement, she responded quickly with a very quiet "Yes, sir," speaking from behind her teacup. I almost dropped my teacup and choked on my tea. I looked around slowly, trying not to appear any way other than calm and confident, before responding, "Are we safe at this moment?" She nodded her head. I slowly stood to my feet.

Over the noise of the machines in the background, I hit the button on my mic and spoke into my radio, "Contact, all people on my position." I looked at my vehicles, knowing there were two of my teammates in the trucks probably struggling to get their kits on while waking up from a nap. "Ma'am, can you tell me about this threat?"

She stood slowly and, with her shoulders slumped forward, said, "There is a man we know who builds bombs in the apartment complex down the road."

I shifted a little to look down the road. Touching my mic again, I said, "We have a potential IED maker. Nick, can you call this up to HQ?" I knew we needed to let everyone know about this in case something bad were to happen and we needed help.

Static came back across the net on my radio. "Roger." I sighed, relieved that Nick had heard me.

The shop owner continued, "A year ago there was a small explosion in his apartment, which is how we know about him."

By this time my team had gathered. "Ma'am, will you give me a minute? And then take me to this person's apartment?" She nodded at both of my inquiries. After seeing her acquiesce, I turned to the guys who were with me that day. "So, here is the dealio. There is a potential IED maker in this apartment complex. I am going to investigate it with Scotty and Ghadir. Should anything happen, we will return to the vehicles and promptly return to the base. If anyone should get hurt, Ham"—I turned to look at the older gentleman with us, who was the senior medic in the area—"it is your call, my brother. The hospital is one hundred feet away, but I give you 100 percent leeway to act."

Nick called the TOC and informed them of the situation.

"Remember, I will fear no evil as I walk through the valley of the shadow of death, because I am the biggest barrel-chested freedom fighter in the valley. Oppressors beware!"

With that horrible speech over, I hoisted my rifle, pulling back on my charging lever to ensure I had a round in the chamber. I would not be caught with a bad guy in my sights and hearing only a *click* because I had failed to verify that I had a round in my chamber.

My team and I walked in single file past the young woman's office and stopped at a glass door. We knocked on the glass door. She opened it. I was the first one to go in. Walking through the door, I raised my rifle and followed it around to the left, seeing that there was a stairwell in front of the door. "Short room," I shouted so the others could hear.

After we had entered the room, flowing into it like water, the last person to have come in said, "All clear." With that, we lowered our weapons. I looked each of my soldiers in the eyes, visually confirming that each was present and accounted for. We took the stairs up to the second floor, having to climb over a dresser that had been thrown down the stairs. We stopped in front of an apartment door. "This isn't the place," the woman told Ghadir. "It is the apartment next to it." I motioned for the team to stack against the door. Ghadir knocked. I stood with Ghadir, who was next to the woman, as an older gentleman opened the door. He smiled upon seeing the woman and Ghadir, and then he was taken aback upon seeing me there with my rifle and smug expression.

The woman started speaking to him. Ghadir leaned in to whisper to me, "She is telling him that we are Americans and that we are here to check on the apartment next to his. She said we want to make sure it is safe and that we want to stop the man from building any more bombs that might hurt or kill more people."

The older man started rubbing his arthritic hands together, which made me a little nervous, but my nervousness went away when he smiled at me, nodded his head, and gestured with his hands for me to enter. Ghadir then told him that we had a whole team so that he would not be surprised as we entered his apartment. Walking into the living room, we saw a couple of teenagers sitting on the floor watching TV who didn't seem to notice us until my guys walked in. We followed the gentleman to a sliding glass window. He opened the door and told us that we would be able to see the bad man's apartment from his balcony, which meant that he'd be able to see us too. I stayed inside the apartment so I didn't attract any attention and peered out of the open door.

"Ghadir, can you ask him when he last saw this individual?" After some conversing, she said that our host hadn't seen the suspected bomb maker in a few weeks. Feeling a little more comfortable thinking that he was not around, I stepped out onto the balcony and quickly surveyed the area. The man pointed to the balcony, about five feet away, and said it was the one belonging to the guy we were looking for. The door was open to the other balcony, so I stepped back inside to talk to my guys.

"Scotty, let's go, my brother. Will you follow me?"

He nodded his head, murmuring, "To Hades and back, sir."

I continued, "I am going over there with Scotty. At the sound of any gunshot, we will return here and get back to our trucks. At no time will anyone cross over unless we don't come out. Is that understood?" Everyone nodded. "Okay, Scotty, let's do some good." Nice—my Kevin Costner quote for the day.

With that, I turned on my heels. Knowing that the greatest warrior on the planet had my back, I took two steps across the balcony and, placing my left foot on the ledge, made the five-foot leap across to the landing on the opposite balcony. Landing on the balls of my feet, I raised my rifle and took a few steps forward. Hearing the thud behind me, I smiled, knowing that Scotty had made it and we were about to do something amazing. This was what I felt I had been placed on earth to do, rid the world of evil.

Scotty and I moved like water from room to room, clearing the entire apartment. As I had suspected, the place was void of anyone. After the entire place was cleared, we unlocked the front door in case we needed a quick exit and admitted the rest of the team. We brought the team over to examine the apartment to make sure we hadn't missed anything. We gleaned a few items from the apartment, but nothing that I thought to be significant, such as an IED. Shannon said we had hit the jackpot and that it might be one of the biggest intel operations of her career. I was happy that we potentially scared the bad guy and prevented him from comfortably building any more IEDs. So, because of a silly half-marathon turkey trot that led to a humanitarian mission based on an overflowing septic system, we were able to corner an IED maker and, thank God, save one life.

19

Education

I will instruct you and teach you in the way which you
should go; I will counsel you with my eye upon you.

—Psalm 32:8

Back in September, I was asked a very important question: "So, why
were you sent here, and how can we help?" Joe had asked me this in
front of a couple of the guys in the tactical operations center (TOC).
I had been perfecting my elevator pitch ever since my assessment
and selection for civil affairs back in 2013, so I knew it like the
back of my hand. It was now time to sell not only myself but also
my capabilities to this Special Forces (SF) team, my new team. I
wanted to hunch my shoulders forward and make a wise crack but
knew that now was not the time for humor, even if it was my coping
mechanism during times of uneasiness. That was only useful during
other circumstances, to make others laugh, and now was not such
a time. Instead, knowing who I was and knowing the organization
I represented, I pushed my shoulders back and tilted my head up
just enough to give off the appearance of utter confidence without
appearing cocky or looking down my nose at this proud branch

of service. "I was sent here to add my civil affairs capability and leadership to the fight by leading a cross-functional team." I looked around the room. Seeing a few blank stares, I knew I needed to further inform them of my capability and what a cross-functional team could do. The need for cross-functional teams is dependent on the situation. It could be a security concern where SF, civil affairs, and psyops need to be combined. It could also be that a small footprint is needed, or the cross-functional team could be designed to have a small footprint based on the commander's guidance.

"Besides our pretty amazing surgical strike capability, I will amaze you with my ability to weed out any potential insurgency in the area of operations [AO]. This will be through means that appear unconventional, which is my area of expertise, as it is yours. I will help you accomplish your mission here and make your team shine as a beacon through means that most other teams will not understand. I only ask that you allow me to operate unhindered. If you have any misgivings or feel uneasy about anything, I will always be more than happy to sit down with you and work through my plans. Also, to help you guys get warm and fuzzy, I would love to take your best soldiers out into the fight with me, especially any of your intel or medical soldiers. This would greatly enhance my capability and would give you reach-back."

Joe was nodding his head. Chief Kyle, next to him, was nodding with a huge grin on his face. That is how I got Chief on my team as a contributing member and an individual whom I wouldn't have left the wire without.

We immediately began working our de-ISIS efforts from any angle we could think of. I pored through any historical document that previous teams had saved on the share drive, spending long hours with Chief Kyle. Kyle and I reached out to other teams in-country to see which of the operations they were doing were working and which were not. It wasn't too long before we found a mission.

While hanging out in the TOC, I overheard Joe talking on the phone with his commander, briefing him on a mission. Joe was planning to go to the southern border of our AO to check on the border guards and see the overall disposition and atmosphere. Since I had not been away from the base yet and was itching to get into sector, when Joe hung up the phone, I rotated my office chair to the right and asked, "Joe, would you mind if I joined you on your mission tomorrow? It couldn't hurt to have another gun for security, and my Arabic to gather further atmospherics."

Much to my excitement, Joe said "Yup" and asked me to fill out the trip ticket for the mission. The ticket was an email that outlined the who, what, when, where, and why. The ticket informed the commanding officer of what we were requesting and gave permission to conduct the mission set in place. This was required to get approval and was sent up to our higher command. I was super pumped to be on a mission.

The mission ended up being a lot of fun. I rode with Chief Kyle, who loved guns and was a joy to chat with for the entire hour drive to the border and back to the base. He was our weapons sergeant and looked like a Viking with his blonde hair and athletic build. He and I made fun of everyone and everything in life. While talking to a few of the villagers, we got a lot of great information that perked up the ears of our higher chain of command and put the location on a sort of watch for the team. Joe commented to me on the way back that he would like to know more about the villages in our area, their sentiment toward coalition forces, and if there were any ISIS sympathies among the people in the countryside. Once back at the base, I talked to Chief Jon about that. It became a focus for us. We filled out our own trip ticket for the next day.

After pulling out the map of our area that my geospatial analysis in Erbil had made for me before I left, I divided it into multiple sectors. Speaking with Kyle, I said that we wanted to get to know the area and the people without being an easy target for the enemy to spot. After developing a basic plan of attack, Kyle and I took it to the roof, walking up the many flights of stairs. With my binoculars, I traced the route that we planned to drive the following day. It was a beautiful day. As I had done many times as a child, I pretended to act out what would happen during the operation. Kyle and I were in a truck driving down the road. We talked through each stop sign and took as good of an account of the route as possible from a rooftop. Along the route we confirmed that we would pass two schools, which were both marked on the map as no-strike locations. I intended to stop at each location and gather information there. Chief Kyle ran through our questionnaire of things that we would ask whomever we met. The fact that we had written the questions ensured that we had a plan and were able to quantify our information. After we collected the information, we could compare it to other areas, developing a potential in-depth understanding of the region based on math rather than emotions.

The route reconnaissance from the rooftop took us about an hour. We didn't want to rush it since our lives could depend on it. We played the what-if game, trying to shoot holes in our well-thought-out plan, until we were both satisfied that we were prepared for the mission. That evening we briefed the team at large, saying that we would be conducting a ground movement to gather information in order to gain a general understanding of the population's sentiments regarding coalition forces and ISIS in our backyard. I excitedly mentioned the soldiers who would be on the mission and kept the smaller team together afterward to run through the nitty-gritty.

Following the smaller team meeting, Ghadir called the Civil Administration of Manbij (CAM) and told them of our intention to visit two of the education centers and their locations. We requested that one of the education administrators be present to escort us through each compound, which was granted.

That night, I fell asleep with a feeling of excitement, knowing that once I awoke, I would be leading a team of some of the best soldiers on the planet on a mission that would become the highlight of my military career. I had finally reached the dream that I had always wanted, to be a Tier 1 team leader. I was doing a job that

Chuck Norris would portray in a movie if someone were to turn this war into an action film.

Waking early the next morning, I threw on my PT shorts and hit the gym. Listening to some manly music, primarily Taylor Swift and Miley Cyrus, I was able to knock out a fantastic workout. After a quick shower to remove the sweat and stink, I grabbed my lightweight body armor, made of soft Kevlar and put it on under my leather jacket, my helmet consisting of hair mousse and my Detroit Tigers baseball cap. I put on a snug pair of blue jeans, then tucked my Glock 19 into my waistband in the appendix carry position. I put my Special Operations Combatives Program dagger on my left hip; clipped my medical aid bag onto my belt behind my back, right next to a thirty-round AR magazine loaded with armor-piercing ammunition, with a few tracer rounds thrown in to point out where I was shooting; and finally grabbed my radio, which I clipped onto my right side for ease of access. I grabbed my truck keys off the vehicle board, also grabbing a truck radio, and headed down to the motor pool beneath our living quarters to prepare my truck for the day's activities.

Once everyone was down in the motor pool, we met in front of my truck. I filled everyone in on what we were doing. "No change to what we briefed last night." With that, I finished things up with the men, then walked to my truck and loaded up. As we drove to the exit, Justin held the door open. I saw him mouth, *Good luck storming the castle. Bye,* as he saw us off the compound. He always made me smile. He was a fine example of a great leader. Leaving the compound, we turned left on the main road and entered a traffic circle. I keyed the mic, saying, "Option two, north," telling everyone we were taking the second exit to the north. Then I switched my radio over to our higher command's frequency and informed them that our element was mobile, which they confirmed, saying they were tracking us.

We drove slowly, taking note of the patterns of life along the way. Children were playing along the street, and shops were open with hawkers displaying their goods, attempting to get us to pull over and purchase their merchandise. I was always leery and amazed that these merchants would approach our vehicles and bang on our windows, knowing full well who we were. We stuck out like a sore thumb with our up-armored SUVs, with a big gun mounted on top of each, and with flashing lights and sirens.

When we arrived at the first school, I overheard Chief Kyle call up our location to our high HQ. I was the first one to step out of the vehicles. I checked the ground around my vehicle and surveyed my surroundings, looking for anything that might harm any of my guys or any of the civilians who were rapidly gathering around our vehicles. Whenever we went somewhere, we quickly became an attraction because everyone wanted to see the Americans. I didn't blame them. We were a sight to behold after so many years of tyranny.

There was no government official, so I started talking with some of the children who were pressing close to me. I pulled a soccer ball from my backpack and started kicking it around with the youngsters while Chief started running through his questions. After about ten minutes, long enough for me to become covered in dripping sweat from attempting to avoid being schooled at soccer by the children, a few adults walked out of the school and waved over to us. I left two soldiers with the trucks as the rest of us approached the three-story building. Our vehicles were safe since we had parked inside a courtyard surrounded by a ten-foot-high wall with concertina wire at the top.

The adults told us that they were refugees from Aleppo and that they were living in the school at this time. They invited us into the school. The first thing I noticed was that there was an ISIS flag front and center of every classroom. The third floor of the school had been destroyed, but the rest of the building seemed mostly intact. I am not an engineer, so I made a mental note to get an engineer in to survey it. When the education administrator, the same guy we had worked with when we learned about the prohibition against girls attending school, finally arrived, super late, he informed us that the school used to have around a thousand students, but since it had been partially destroyed, these kids had not been back to school in three years. I asked what it would take to get them back in school, and he said it would cost about one hundred thousand dollars to remove the rubble from the third floor and thereby render the school safe for class. While he spoke, I thought about how I might come up with that kind of money. Knowing that there is always a way to a yes, I thanked him for helping us better understand what was going on in the area. We had found out that there was a very small ISIS presence in the area, but the people were still afraid of them, which was why ISIS flags remained in the school.

After talking with the people, we determined that if we were to remove the flags, it would bolster the local population's morale and their confidence in the coalition, while helping force a negative attitude toward ISIS. Working toward a solution to getting the thousand students off the streets, where they were vulnerable to recruitment, and back into school, I contacted the Department of State (DoS) to see what they recommended.

Patrick was my point of contact with DoS. Being a person who always had an amazing grasp of the goings-on within the region, he recommended that we not pay to fix the school even though we were the ones who had dropped the bomb that destroyed the third floor. Instead, he knew of movable containers that the military could relocate to serve as temporary classrooms. We worked together to make this happen. A few weeks later, I was sitting down with the government and the military leadership. As the buildings were being transported, I was excited to see the procession and hear from the people that they were excited to see the military working with the government, not only to keep the people safe but also to secure a safe and prosperous future for the children of Syria. Not only did we provide classrooms for one thousand children, ensuring that they would no longer be vulnerable to ISIS recruiters, but also we enhanced the population's feelings toward the local government and military, while delegitimizing ISIS's influencing. We also purchased about fifty gallons of paint and painted over each ISIS flag in the destroyed building. The only negative outcome of the operation was that I never got a chance to get my soccer ball back—and my pride had gone along with it.

20

Real Civil Affairs Stuff

In the cover of your presence you hide them from the plots of men, you store them in your shelter from the strife of tongues.

—Psalm 31:20

The last assessment I did was at a school right next door to the Ramadan Hiju Elementary School, which was once the ISIS headquarters/jail but had been turned back into a school. After we worked to get girls back into school, the education department wanted to show us that they were making good on their part to provide instruction to the young women of the region while we provided security, making sure the schools were safe from ISIS interference. We walked from our vehicles, which were parked in front of the school, where the kids peered out of the windows at us, and headed through the front gate. Everyone who was on this mission was wearing civilian clothes, which was the norm for every mission I oversaw that occurred in the city. This mission was different from most in terms of personnel as we had with us our new combat camera soldier—the position had been rebranded and was no longer a part of the former Public Affairs Branch—a young woman named

Zoe. She was by far the youngest soldier on our compound, about half the age of the next-youngest teammate, but she was able to hold her own with us. As we walked into the school, the children rushed to us, which was normal. I was used to being the center of attention, not only the teacher's attention but also the students'. I usually had a few gifts, and this time I tossed out a couple of soccer balls for the kids to play with. Different from other times, the kids gathered around Zoe and tried to pull her into the courtyard with them. Ghadir laughed at the spectacle and told me that the elementary students thought that Zoe was their age. We each laughed at that. She was their height, and being from Puerto Rico, her tan skin made her blend in well with them. Many times in the near future I would have to talk to people on Zoe's behalf, explaining that she was not an Arab and didn't speak Arabic even though she looked more the part than I did. I extricated her from the children, and we conducted a quick assessment of the school.

Sitting down with a couple of the teachers, I asked them what the largest problem they faced was. They responded that they didn't have basic school supplies such as paper and writing equipment. These were things that the State Department was interested in supplying, so I continued to listen and write down their requests in my notebook. One of the teachers showed us a bathroom where he had spent three weeks as a prisoner when ISIS was in charge. As we were commenting that we couldn't believe he had fit in the small space, let alone be in there for that length of time, he told us that he feared ISIS would regain a stronghold on the community through the children this winter, especially if they were not able to keep the kids in school. At the current place and time, none of the windows had glass, and none of the rooms had heaters, so he feared that none of the parents would make their kids go to school because it would be too cold during the winter. Then ISIS would be able to gain access to the children and gain influence over them—and thus gain a foothold in the community while the kids were not in school. I commented that this was a project that I would like to look at because I didn't like ISIS and didn't want them to be able to exert any type of influence ever again in this town.

After the assessment, I compiled my notes and sent up my report. Even though I had been on the ground for a couple of months, I still had not received my operational funds (OpFund), which would have allowed me to purchase the needed supplies with ease. Without the OpFund, I had to get creative on funding, so I reached out to the State Department, who said they would help with the school supplies. I then worked with my roommate and his psyops team on how to pay for renovating the school. I typed up the project nomination. Once it was approved, we drove to the school, where we paid a contractor to emplace windows to keep out the winter weather. After paying the contractor, we drove downtown with the education director and our government administrator. We parked about a quarter of a mile from the store we were planning on going to. I walked with my team through the narrow streets to a commodity shop. I must have walked past this shop a dozen times while shopping with Ghadir for food, but I had never stopped. This time we stopped, and we began negotiations for fifty oil-burning heaters. The price was not set as we are used to in the United States, so we were able to get a much cheaper price, which meant we purchased a far greater number of heaters than what we had originally intended. The additional heaters would be sent to another school to serve a similar purpose. After the negotiation was completed, I stepped out of the shop. Nick handed the money to Ghadir, who passed it to the shop owner. After the sale, the shop owner stepped outside and shook my hand, thanking me for my business and telling me I had helped make the city a better place. Zoe snapped a quick photo of the scene before we headed back to our vehicles.

For whatever reason, we hadn't left our vehicles running. It would become standard operating procedure (SOP) to do so from this moment on, until the end of the deployment. We mounted up after a quick patrol brief and then sat on the side of the road because my truck refused to turn over. I started to sweat when the key fob seemed not to work. I was not too fond of these electric starting vehicles, and it really bothered me that of all the times our truck couldn't start, this had to be one of them. We were stuck on the side of the road. At least we were in the safe part of town; there was good security because the local police department was just a block away. We made a few phone calls, notifying the TOC that the truck wasn't starting, and they started running through different ways to get it started. Rather than sit there pulling my hair out, I grabbed a couple of guys, and Ghadir, and recommended that we go for a walk to maximize the use of our time rather than sit waiting in the truck for a solution to our problem. We knew this area well, so we walked a few feet down the road to a nice spot where there was a great little pizza place I knew. When stressed out, why not get some comfort food? So that is what I did. After I had bought enough pizza for everyone, we hiked back to the vehicles. My truck was running. We ate in silence. I thanked God that the truck was running. Chief Kyle had found the solution. I owed him a huge one.

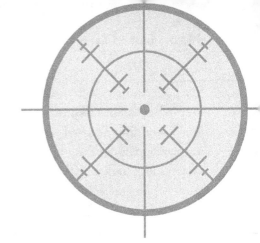

21

Operation Finding Gold—Maybe

My fruit is better than gold, even fine gold,
and my yield than choice silver.

—Proverbs 8:19

In December, as my team and I were sitting in a conference room with the commander of the Manbij Military Council (MMC), he made sure to let us know that if we found any of ISIS's gold, we should share it with him because, he said, it would go a long way toward healing the land and the wounds that the people of Manbij had suffered at the hands of ISIS. Not in the fortune-making business, I didn't quite hear what he said, except that there was a way to heal the people's wounds. But someone else had overheard exactly what he said and had asked for further clarification. "There is supposedly five hundred million dollars in gold bullion that ISIS stole when they overtook a portion of Iraq. The gold was last reported here in Manbij, and then it disappeared." He believed that it was buried in our town or at one of the ISIS headquarters. That added an air of excitement to our operations but didn't become the sole focus for us. I know that that much money would have helped improve our living conditions, but I was happy where I was in life.

I soon found myself deep in the underground caverns with the team, mapping out the tunnels using nothing more than a compass and a laser range finder. By this time, we had requested help from my intel guys, who were in Erbil, and had Levi and Ben on the ground. I was very happy to have those two with me. Walking around underground with my guys was a great deal of fun. We tried to do the whole operation with night vision goggles, but without any light, they didn't work, so we used our flashlights—and used our pistols for protection, with our knives for backup. I felt confident that we had mapped out most of the ISIS tunnels beneath our compound leading into the town and into the countryside. ISIS operatives had spent the larger part of the decade of their occupation here digging out these tunnels. I knew this because there were miles upon miles of tunnels that were wide enough for a couple of guys to walk side by side through and tall enough for me to stand up in. I am taller than just about every Syrian. As the ISIS tunnels were not panning out and we had no luck finding any gold, we got a lead from the education department.

Supposedly, there was a bathroom that ISIS had welded up before leaving. It had not been opened since. Written on the door was "al'algham" or, in English, "mines." The department asked if we would take a look inside. While doing the premission briefing, Ghadir said that the bathroom was dangerous because it could be booby-trapped. Being the real mature person in the group, I had to laugh. She ended up slapping me, which I deserved, her knowing what I was thinking. Then we ran through the mission brief.

The day was one of the coldest ones there was during the whole deployment. I didn't want to get out of the truck. We parked around the corner, in front of the school. Once the Syrian Democratic Forces (SDF) had quarantined the school, we met up with the education director and the school's administrator, who showed us the bathroom, which was separated from the school by about fifty feet. At this moment there were five bathroom stalls for about fifteen hundred students. If we could open the other half, then they could open their doors to another fifteen hundred students, thus denying ISIS the ability to influence these children who were currently out on the street and out of school. Jarod and Darius, explosive ordnance disposal noncommissioned officers (EOD guys) who were in the Marine Corps, got to work climbing on the building. I always included them in my mission planning in case there were any explosives or traps. They could clear an area such as a minefield or a building very quickly, rendering it safe. I had never seen two guys do this job so well. They started drilling holes through windows to look inside, and finally they grinded through the welded-shut door. Trusting entirely in their professionalism, I cringed just a little when they hit the door with a sledgehammer. Once the door was opened, I took the first step inside. Jarod said it was clear, so I walked in, showing that I trusted him. There was no gold, so that was good. I had worked with the civil administration to make sure they were prepared to renovate the bathroom once we opened it. A few days later the bathroom was cleaned and ready for the children to use. I commented to Ghadir that I was glad that there were no snakes in this stinking place, as otherwise we would have had to kill them. Scotty wasn't there this time, so it would have been a much louder *boom* without his suppressor. It was another seemingly simple mission where we did a little work that most people wouldn't think would make an impact on the war, but at the end of the day it had made a great impact, lasting perhaps decades, on the lives of between one thousand and fifteen hundred children who were able to return to school, and their families. ISIS could no longer prey upon these children, and the government was able to appear in control. This gave the Syrian government the ability to exert its influence and show that it placed a high priority on security through something as simple as a bathroom. Being blessed with wonderful bowels and being lactose-intolerant, I regard bathrooms as important. I couldn't imagine what it would be like if I didn't have one around when I had to go.

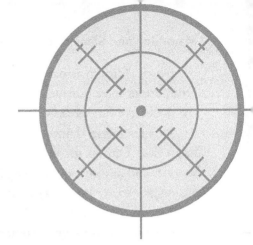

22

Operation Finding Bombs

> But the Lord is faithful. He will establish you
> and guard you against the evil one.
>
> —2 Thessalonians 3:3

During my first two weeks in Manbij, there were a couple of explosions that warranted our manning of all battle positions for longer than an hour. While our soldiers manned their positions, Joe, Ghadir, and I spoke with our partner force to determine if our assistance was required to render aide or chase down ISIS and help provide security. With our arms loaded with equipment, and while fumbling with guns and ammo and donning equipment, we commonly sang a song from a show that we loved, *How I Met Your Mother*. As the character Marshall Eriksen from the show sings in one episode, "I said a-bang, bang, bangity-bang." It would always elevate our heart rate and get our feet running. Each time led to a stand-down, which was disappointing for the soldiers, but it stood as a testament to the training given by Joe's team and the capability of our partner force to arrive on the scene of a horrible terrorist attack. Our partner force provided security and medical aid and got us off the site before further assistance was needed.

Joe's team had trained our partner force very well. I was very impressed. During my operations, whether in the city gathering supplies and information or going into sector, one question I started asking next to my "Are we safe?" question was, "Are there any bombs nearby that could hurt your friends or family?" One such day while we were walking through the bazaar, an older woman overheard me speaking with a shop owner while I was stuffing a pizza down my throat. She tugged on my leather jacket sleeve, drawing my attention instantly because I didn't like being touched. My jacket was very important to me. I had purchased the jacket on a deployment in Jordan, and after having worn it during two deployments, I noticed that it was very difficult to rip. I counted it as a form of soft body armor, so when someone pulled on it, I didn't like it.

The woman spoke to Ghadir and told her that there was a bomb a few stores down in a medical clinic where she normally took her baby. I asked her to take us to the clinic, which she hesitated to do. Seeing her look at my pizza, I offered her some of the food we were purchasing, which she refused. She relented and said she would take us only if I gave her toddler boy a cake smothered in Nutella, which made him start speaking a thousand words a second. The woman appeared to be homeless. I slipped the store owner a few additional bills and told him to take care of the little guy if he asked for more food. The boy reminded me of my son. I hated seeing any young child go hungry. It weighed heavy on my heart and made me miss my wife and son. I would have to return to this restaurant to see if I could help further.

We walked down the road and entered a medical clinic. I thanked the woman, who thanked us over and over for the kindness that we had shown to her and were showing to her country. I asked if there was anything else that she could tell us. Ghadir proceeded to ask her further questions about ISIS and anything that might harm her or her son in the area. We told her that we would return to the area, adding that if she needed anything, she should get ahold of us. I made sure to give her my business card, then I turned my attention to a receptionist in the clinic. The receptionist was probably wondering who we were walking into her medical clinic with a homeless woman and her son while carrying a bunch of guns.

I placed my elbows on the counter and smiled at the young woman behind the desk. It was a smile that I knew would either get me whatever I wanted or get us kicked out instantly. "Good morning, ma'am. I am Captain Jon Turnbull, a United States soldier. I heard that there might be a bomb in the basement here, and I would like to see the basement if that is possible. My guys are professionals and might be able to make it safe." Knowing my Arabic was not the best, I watched her face as I spoke, looking for any signs. I saw her nod a couple of times. At the last sentence, she stood up and walked away from the desk. I turned to my left and looked at Ghadir.

Like a condescending teacher, Ghadir patted me on my left shoulder and said, "Good job, Jon. Most of your words were wrong, but not wrong enough that she didn't understand you." A moment later a man walked into view with the woman and motioned for us to follow him. He ushered us down a stairwell into a basement. It was dark; the floor was made of sand. In the middle of the floor was a circular tube about the size of a PVC pipe, four inches in diameter, sticking out of the ground about two feet. This bomb was much smaller than the one in our building. I snapped a bunch of pictures with my cell phone and asked the doctor if we could return later in the week with my explosive ordnance disposal (EOD) team, to which he nodded excitedly.

Walking back outside, I was happy to breathe in the clean air and, honestly, happy to be away from the boom-boom thing. The doctor told me that there were about five hundred individuals in the building that was housing the bomb. If the bomb were to explode, it would kill many, and the damage would cripple the one building that thousands of people in the city use. Not only was this a medical facility, but also it was an apartment building. There were restaurants in the complex as well. I made sure to take note of this. After thanking the doctor for his hospitality, I asked him not to go near that thing and said we would be back shortly.

The mission was a lock. I sent up a recommendation after talking to Jarod and Darius, our EOD experts, and recommended the removal of the explosive. Joe's team took my recommendation one step further, which was typical of Joe. Rather than just make it a coalition operation, Joe wanted it to become a training mission for the SDF. I was thrilled that he thought the way he did and had been able to come up with a way to kill two birds with one stone. Our task force approved the mission packet. A few short days later, we had security of the area with the roads surrounding the building blocked, shutting traffic down, just to protect everyone.

It was a beautiful day. I walked up and down the street talking with patrons and shop owners, recommending that they take a few short hours off while we took care of "some stuff." EOD hadn't been down in the hole for more than a few minutes before a call came across my radio that medical attention was needed. With my heart racing, I shifted my gun in my hand and walked briskly to the entrance of the building to make sure everything was okay and offer to help in any way that I could. Jarod, the lead EOD NCO, was walking out with our lead medic guiding him by his elbow. I walked over to my truck with the duo. Jarod sat down in the back seat with Ham leaning over him. Ham talked while he worked on Jarod as if it were an exercise. I kept my eyes open, looking up and down the street, to make sure no one got the drop on us.

While keeping watch, I heard Ham say that Jarod had hit his head on a low overhang. I tried very hard not to laugh as Ham gave Jarod a couple of stitches and cleaned the blood from his forehead, before sending him back down to the basement. Our linguist of the day, Ubed, took Jarod down. I stuck around, helping Ham clean everything up. A few seconds later, Ubed was standing next to our truck, holding his head. I chuckled, knowing that Ubed had hit his head on the exact same spot. I told him that at least Ham had had some practice with Jarod.

I wanted to see this low-hanging ceiling that was taking out my guys, so I left the truck and went down to the bomb. I didn't hit my head but found something far worse. As I rounded the corner of the basement to the room where the bomb was, I saw something that made my heart stop. One of the SDF soldiers whom our EOD guys were training had a pickax and was swinging it right next to the bomb to unearth the explosive. Not being an EOD specialist, I had to trust my guys entirely, but still I had to wonder if Jarod hadn't hit his head a little too hard. I asked him, and he said that the bomb was still live but the ax wouldn't set it off. I was glad for that. They kept swinging away.

Not feeling comfortable with what was going on, I decided not to stay down there and watch them "play." I returned to the sunlight. Before too long, Jarod and Darius emerged with the SDF EOD team and a huge bomb, which they placed in the back of a trailer that we had hooked up behind my truck.

While they were working on the bomb, I was walking around. Seeing them swinging the ax, I had to check a few things. About one hundred feet away was our helicopter landing zone, which would be used in case of any medical evacuations. I walked over to it. The site was a soccer field surrounded by a ten-foot wall and bleachers. There was a smaller soccer field made of turf where about twenty kids were playing soccer. When I walked over to the fence, a couple of adults came out and greeted me. I asked the common questions, and they asked if I could put turf on a large soccer field. Answering my questions, they pointed at something that they said was very dangerous. I didn't know what it was, so I walked up to it. Who doesn't walk up to something that people say is dangerous?

The item that they said was dangerous was a series of tubes from which ISIS used to fire rockets. I was fascinated with the device and marked it down in my notebook with a quickly sketched grid. The SDF also noted its location. I asked them to remove it from the children's soccer field because it remained as a symbol of ISIS. They removed it the next day, then took it to the SDF's police headquarters, which we would see in a few weeks when we introduced the new team in December. Once the bomb was safely removed from the basement, I thanked the doctors in the clinic and told them that everything was safe. I handed out my business card and told them that if they found anything else that could hurt them, they should call me. I would do what I could to help.

We drove to a preapproved EOD site, where our guys taught the SDF how to dispose of ordnance. This site was in view of the Tay-Tay Memorial Grain Silo. We had to coordinate with everyone so there wasn't mass hysteria with the big boom.

A few weeks later while out in sector checking out medical clinics, I was told about a few poor children who had stepped on a land mine and were killed. I told the nurse that I wanted to help, and she said there was a way I could do so. There was a large bomb that could kill a lot of kids, and it was right next to the road. She told us where it was, and we loaded up the trucks and drove to the site. Jarod and Darius walked onto a field and looked at the bomb, which resembled a large water heater on its side.

While they were examining the explosive, I stood at the edge of a field and looked at what was around. There was a large compound nearby with about twenty kids playing. Seeing us, they ran out to see what was going on. To keep them away from Jarod and Darius while they worked, I attracted the kids to me using an ancient method called candy. While they munched on the sweets that I carried with me everywhere to keep my hangry monster at bay, I asked them about the big shiny object. Apparently, the big object had flown overhead and fallen out of the sky a few years ago, landing in the field behind me. There was another one that had exploded, but this one hadn't. The farmer had dug it up and dragged it to the road because he needed to plant his crops. It had been sitting in the road for the past two years. I gave the kids a couple of soccer balls to perpetuate the stereotype of the Civil Affairs Regiment, and then we mounted up, telling the youngsters to stay away from the bomb. Jarod and Darius said that they thought the bomb was inert and was harmless. They couldn't be certain because the writing on it was in Russian. Their report got a lot of attention because of this.

To make Manbij safer, we had to take care of a lot of bombs during our deployment. We were very successful in doing so. Jarod and Darius saved thousands of limbs and prevented the deaths of hundreds of kids through their ability to stay calm while digging up a bomb and defusing it. I was impressed by them every time. They did what I couldn't do, that is for sure, and I appreciated them, as I still do, as teammates. Jarod and Darius, thank you for showing me that I didn't need to jump over the candlestick, but instead just blow it out, or else walk around it so I didn't burn my bum. God bless you two. You will always be remembered as heroes of Manbij.

23

Talking to Samantha

Train up a child in the way he should go; even
when he is old, he will depart from it.

—Proverbs 22:6

One of the hardest parts about the job I was doing was not being able
to tell my wife details about my missions or my daily routines and
activities. My wife has a superpower though, I believe, because she
always knows what is going on even if I do not tell her. I was busy
working getting ready to prepare for our next mission, and whenever
I had a spare moment, I was texting with Samantha. I felt bad I was
not able to call and text her as much as I wanted to, so any moment
I had to call home, I tried. This time our conversation was a little
different from others we had had. I missed her and missed my son
a lot this day. Samantha was texting me, telling me about how our
son was doing in school. I didn't know if I should laugh, be upset,
or be proud—or be all at the same time. Samantha had been called
to the school our son attended because he got in a fight with another
boy in his class. The children were out to recess, and being in North
Carolina, the weather was warm considering it was only January. It

was time to go back to class, so Ian's teacher told the students to run to the fence surrounding the playground and grab their jackets and lunch boxes so they could head back to class.

Our son is very small. He is the youngest in his grade, but Samantha and I decided to enroll him into school early because he was extremely smart for his age. Just because he is small, though, doesn't mean he isn't a very fast runner. As the story goes, when sprinting to the fence line, Ian was the first to arrive at the finish line. His friend in his class, not liking the fact that he had lost, decided to reward Ian's accomplishment by slapping him across the face and calling him a cheater. The teacher must have missed this because all she saw was Ian teaching this other young boy how to fight properly. Instead of crying, Ian held his fist up and said, "You don't slap people across the face! You punch them like this!" while holding his fist up next to his own face. He wasn't going to punch the boy but instead was teaching him (in my opinion) a valuable life lesson. That was when Samantha got the phone call and was told to come get him from school. She texted me. Honestly, I was so proud of Ian that I didn't know how to handle the situation, especially with being completely across the world, so I told Samantha that she was a wonderful mom who knew how to handle it. If I remember correctly, she signed Ian out of school early and treated him to a McDonald's Happy Meal.

We texted back and forth a little more, and for some reason I felt the need to tell Samantha something I knew I was not allowed to do. On the last four deployments I had been on, she never knew what I was doing, but in my heart, I felt it was important to tell her this time. I explained to her that ISIS had moved into our area and was after us. They knew why we were in Manbij and what we were doing. To ease her mind, I told her we were going to be heading into town in the morning to set up security cameras and try to capture their movements and locations. The last thing we wanted was for any of us to get hurt. Knowing my wife, I figured that surely she had started worrying. I hoped that my telling her this would help alleviate some of her anxiousness. I told Samantha I loved her and Ian very much, adding that I would text her again after I got back.

I went to bed and was very excited to wake up in the morning. Chief Jon, Shannon, Scotty, Devin, Ghadir, and I were about to go on our next mission. Joining us on this run were two guys named Joe and Clark, who added to our security. Little did I know, my life was about to change forever.

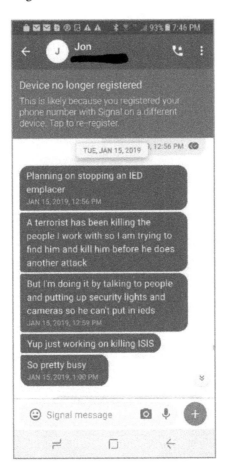

24

Boom

January 16, 2019

Greater love has no one than this, that he
lay down his life for his friends.

—John 15:3

Thinking, talking, and even writing about this day is very difficult
for me. I remember a lot of what occurred, but any gaps in my
memory I filled after hearing my teammates' story of what happened
and reviewing reports of the explosion. Unfortunately, the majority
of the information in the reports is classified, so I have to be careful
in recounting the event, so I don't mention anything that I am not
supposed to. The Pentagon has ensured that everything mentioned
in the following is unclassified and accurate.

Standing grouped together in front of the Palace of Princes
restaurant, and next door to one of the schools we had rendered
nonlethal aid to, after another very successful mission in downtown
Manbij to remove the stain of ISIS, I told everyone they had done
a good job on the mission and informed them that our patrol

was to head back to base. Standing in front of my armored white Toyota Land Cruiser with the number 3 taped on the side, I looked into the eyes of each of my teammates to ensure they were attentive to my instruction. I told them, "I will be driving the lead vehicle with Scotty as my truck commander, navigator, and DJ. In my truck, there is a lot of sensitive equipment, from our radios to our weapons, but the most important thing inside the vehicle besides me is"—I paused, looking around to build up the suspense. Locking eyes with our assigned linguist, I continued with my patrol briefing—"Ghadir. In the event anything renders my vehicles immobile, make sure the trail vehicle pulls up on the safe side and you nerds in it cross-load men, weapons, and equipment into your vehicle. Then ensure that we make it back to the base as quickly as possible. Time is the most important asset we have, so no lingering on the spot—no matter how badly we want to get into a gunfight."

With Joe and Devin to my side, I finished speaking, looking Scotty directly in the eyes, knowing that he was the most likely one among us to get pulled into a gunfight. He was the most lethal member of our team with more time behind a rifle than the rest of us combined. He nodded in understanding. I wished everyone good luck, telling them to mount up like the old cavalryman I was. Then I turned to my left to return to my own vehicle.

As I turned, I saw that Shannon's blonde hair was done up on top of her head. She had a slight smirk on her face from knowing that she had just completed a very successful operation that would make not only her organization but also the whole navy proud of her. I saw Jon smiling with the knowledge that the mission we were on was a success. Then I saw Scotty with his hand on his pistol.

As I turned, my ears picked up the worst sound I could have heard while in theater. "Jon!" Ghadir shouted. She had recognized a threat to my team and the civilians who had intermingled with our group. Directly behind her was Chief, Scotty, and Shannon; however, behind them, there was something that wasn't not right. As I turned to look, I saw Scotty turn to go to his vehicle and a middle-aged male fill the gap he had just vacated. At present, I still do not know the exact details of the attacker, so I will refer to him as a demon. In the seconds during which I moved to lift my firearm to engage this demon, the demon detonated his suicide vest and my world went black.

Boom!

In that moment, that coward killed Shannon, Scotty, Ghadir, and Chief Jon. Dozens of civilians who surrounded us, three American soldiers, my linguist, and five others who worked with us—gone. Twenty-five people gone for no reason other than one selfish demon didn't like that we were trying to make the small city we were in a better place. ISIS found out about what we were doing in the area and had spent a month preparing for this attack before we could remove them from the region, without our knowing. We were making an impact in Manbij. Everything was good there. Schools were opening for the children, hospitals were improved, bombs were being removed throughout the city, emergency transportation was now mobile, and power and water had been restored to the city. The evil that exists in these ISIS fighters is something none of us will ever know. But ISIS was there to fight good with evil. I am thankful that each of my teammates died instantly without pain. However, I was lying on the ground wedged under my truck, along with the three remaining teammates of mine Clark, Joe, and Devin, who somehow had lived and were able to stand up, find me, and get me out of the rubble. I remember only pain so intense that it knocked me straight into unconsciousness. My world turned completely dark.

This darkness became something I still cannot describe. Little did I know, but when I eventually woke up again, this pain would become the type of pain that was so emotionally damaging, I wouldn't wish it on anyone.

May you forever rest in peace, my friends. I will see you again one day, and it will be the greatest reunion heaven will ever experience. I love you each very much.

SCOTT A. WIRTZ | JONATHAN R. FARMER ARMY CHIEF WARRANT OFFICER 2 | SHANNON M. KENT CHIEF PETTY OFFICER | GHADIR TAHER

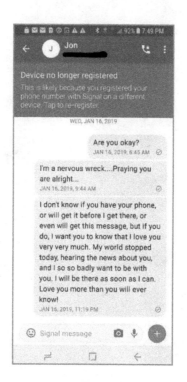

 42 minutes ago

6 civilians killed and 19 injured in downtown Manbij. Explosion coincided with the passage of a patrol of US forces

Manbij, Aleppo Governorate

25

Waking Up Samantha

Therefore, what God has joined together, let no one separate.

—Mark 10:9

At 0630, back at home, Samantha was without a doubt awakened by something, which could have only occurred because of our love. She was sound asleep but sat straight up in bed because she swore she had heard something crash downstairs. While sitting up, she told me, she couldn't describe what was happening. There was a large ray of sunshine shining into our bedroom from our master bathroom window that, she said, was brighter than any she had ever seen before, but in that moment, she felt at peace considering she had just been scared awake. Her phone began buzzing. Reaching for her phone on the nightstand, she grabbed it, wondering who would be calling or texting so early in the morning. Much to her surprise, it wasn't anybody. It was something much worse than she had anticipated. She had an app on her phone that allowed her to get news from any area she chose. With me being in Syria, she had it set to alert her to Syrian news. If anyone sent out a tweet or made some other social media post, this app would pick it up and send out any information that was available if the tweet or post was shared more than three times. Samantha, looking at her phone, saw a post that simply read, "Six civilians killed and nineteen injured in downtown Manbij. Explosion coincided with the passage of patrol of US forces." This was followed by security camera footage.

Samantha remembers watching the video, crying, and telling herself, *There is no way anybody could have survived that.* She then remembered I was in Manbij. My wife has had the worst year of her life (I will get to that in a little bit), but on January 16, 2019, she had to do everything within her power to ensure her heart would not shatter completely. She sat in our bed alone, her heart racing and hands shaking, and prayed. She begged God to spare my life, and she prayed for the families who were going to be having soldiers and strangers coming to their homes today. She texted me on an app called Signal, and simply said, "Please tell me that you are all right." She waited to see two blue check marks, which would mean that I had received and seen her message, for almost an hour, without receiving anything. She knew right then that she was going to be one of the spouses who must live their worst nightmare. She texted our closest friends and families and told them, "There was an explosion where Jon was. I have texted him but haven't heard anything yet. I will let you know as soon as I hear anything. Please just pray."

Samantha got up and got our son ready for school, feeling as if she was going to be sick at any moment. They got in the car, and Samantha did the one thing that she always did when she was upset about something: she turned music on. With the radio up in the car, trying to distract herself with the music, she let the tears flow and tried not to let Ian know that anything was wrong. Samantha has attended church her entire life. When she was young, her father went into ministry. She has always been proud to say she was a PK, a.k.a. a preacher's kid. Living next door to her grandparents, she rarely missed a Sunday morning or Sunday evening church service, and Wednesday nights were always her favorite times of the week, mostly because it meant going to church and hanging out with her teenage friends. She had always heard of people hearing God speak to them and of how they could remember the exact dates and times when they encountered God. Even Samantha never understood what that meant, although she always longed to hear God speaking to her. She can now say that on January 16, 2019, at 7:40 in the morning, she not only heard God speak to her but also felt him in every fiber of her body. She simply prayed, "God, please just let me know you are real. Please just show me in some way that I am going to be okay. If you decide to take my husband today, will you just let me know that Ian and I will be all right? I know that your plans are always greater than my own, but I just want an answer. I need you more than ever to show me you are here with me." As soon as she had prayed that, she realized that the song "Thy Will" by Hillary Scott and the Scott Family was playing on the radio.

Through the song, Samantha heard God saying, "I know that this is hurting you, and I know you don't understand what I am doing. Your heart is going to hurt through this a lot, but I will be right beside you through all of it. Do not worry, my child, because whatever happens today, I've got this. Put your faith and your trust in me."

Samantha ended her prayer by saying, "Whatever happens today, your will be done. I'm trusting that you will help me no matter what. Amen."

As they arrived at the school, Sam hugged Ian goodbye and told him that she loved him more than anything. She also told him that our very dear friend Rob would probably be picking him up after school, so Ian shouldn't worry if he saw Rob at the end of the day; Samantha would be home when Ian got there. Sam said a quick prayer and told Ian to have a good day at school.

Driving away that morning, she told me later, was worse than the very first day of kindergarten. She almost called Ian back just to come home with her. The last thing she wanted was to be alone.

Sam got home, and since she still hadn't heard anything, she showered, knowing she had better get ready for the day. Then she started cleaning the house, in between texting anyone and everyone she knew at Fort Bragg. She called her friend Ashleigh, and Ashleigh gave Sam a little peace of mind, reminding her that she probably couldn't get ahold of me because the cell phone towers were blacked out or I was probably swamped with work, but she promised Sam that she would try to get ahold of me and find anything out she could. At this point, Samantha became frantic and called the last person she thought would have an answer, namely, Chief Michael's former wife, Rebecca. Sam didn't have Michael's phone number, so this was her only option. If anyone would have known something, it would have been him.

At the time, Rebecca didn't know anything, but she told Sam to meet her in town and suggested they could get some lunch and wait together until they heard anything. Sam was not hungry, but she went anyway. They met at Panera.

Rebecca said to Sam, "I hate to ask, but could we go somewhere else? I really would like to try out a different restaurant, but it is across town." Sam had a feeling that something was up and that Rebecca was stalling for time, but she played along and agreed. They drove to the other place and ate lunch. Sam showed Rebecca the video of the explosion. They stuck around for about an hour. Rebecca's phone rang. She stepped outside to take a phone call from Michael. Sitting alone, Sam knew in that moment that she was a widow. Much to her surprise, Rebecca, having come back in, said, "Sorry. That was Mike. I don't know why I went outside. I should have stayed here. Still no word. So, what is next on the agenda?! Do you want to go across the street and get some Dairy Queen?" Sam told her she wasn't in the mood but that she would go. She just had to make it quick because she had to get back home and get Ian from school. Sam could tell that something was wrong, but she kept her hopes up anyway.

At the Dairy Queen, Rebecca and Sam quickly ate their ice cream, then Sam told Rebecca that she had to leave. Rebecca told Sam she needed to use the restroom. Before Sam knew it, Rebecca had pulled her into the restroom with her. Being weirded out, Sam told Rebecca, "*Please* just tell me. Is my husband alive or not?"

Rebecca gave Sam a huge hug and, holding back tears, told her, "Sam, I am not supposed to say anything to you, and Michael is probably going to get in a *lot* of trouble for telling me. I do not know how you have known all day, because we just found out, but Jon was in the explosion. He somehow is one of three survivors. For now, he is alive. That is what we know." Sam fell into the wall behind her and cried. Thankfully, Rebecca pulled her somewhat back into reality and told her that they needed to get home because the soldiers from Fort Bragg were going to be on their way to their houses.

Sam made it back to our car and got herself home with Rebecca following behind her. She called my father and then my father-in-law on the drive home and simply told them I had been at the site of the explosion and was still alive, but they needed to get down to North Carolina as soon as possible. Then she called Rob's wife, Trina, and asked for help getting Ian. Crying through the phone, Trina told Sam to get home and not to worry about Ian. She and Rob were on their way to get him and would meet Sam and Rebecca at Sam's and my house.

Back at home, Sam and Rebecca waited and waited and waited. By now it was three in the afternoon. Ian came home with Rob and Trina. Seeing the sadness on Sam's face, Ian asked what was wrong. Sam, having been dreading this moment, told him, "You know how we pray for Daddy's safety every night? Well, a very bad guy hurt Daddy today. He is alive for now, but we don't know what is wrong yet. Daddy just needs prayers right now." Ian, understanding how important this was, prayed a prayer for me, for which I bless God every day. With Rob, Trina, Rebecca, and our pastor Mike together in our living room, at half past four Sam heard the doors on a car outside shut. She knew it was time to face every military spouse's worst nightmare—the knock on the door.

I am forever grateful for the friends who were surrounding my wife and son at that moment. Trina reassured Sam that there were four soldiers, which was a good thing, and not just two. Also, they were wearing their camo uniforms, not their dress blues. They sat Sam down in the kitchen. She was prepared for the worst possible news. My boss, Sergeant Major, our chaplain Jordan, and my good friend Aaron came into the kitchen and, with sadness on their faces, let Sam know that I was alive but that they weren't hopeful that I was going to live for even twenty-four hours. Sam still, to this day, doesn't remember much of their conversation. The only thing she heard was "Jon took the majority of the explosion to his face and chest. He lost his right eye, and they are doing everything they can to save the left." She felt as if she had become a student in the *Peanuts* movies, hearing nothing but mumbling after that. Nothing else mattered in that moment to Sam. I was alive, but I was also blind.

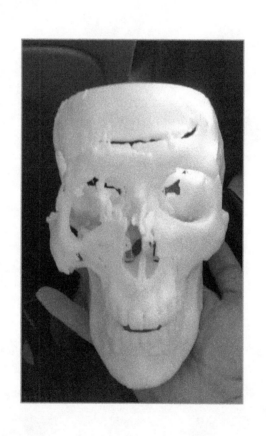

26

God Sends Devin

For he will command his angels concerning you to guard
you in all your ways; they will lift you up in their hands,
so that you will not strike your foot against a stone.

—Psalm 91:11–12

The following is the account of one of the other survivors of that
fateful day, an individual whom I credit with the saving of my life.
I still suffer from postblast amnesia and remember little from that
day. The following account is from what Devin has told me:

There were a couple of amazing things that occurred during
the explosion. First and foremost, four Americans had been killed
directly in front of me, and five soldiers from the Syrian Democratic
Forces had been killed behind me. From what I was told about my
exact location during the blast, I can only describe as a "hand of
God" moment. In an explosion, there is an invisible blast field, then a
fireball. The only reason I survived, I believe, was that I was directly
in the middle of both horrific places. Those who had been killed
were in the blast portion, and Devin and Joe were in the fireball.
I was the only one in the middle. I thank God for preserving my

life. I attribute my being alive to nothing other than him—and to my having made Psalm 91 my daily prayer. I tell everyone I know how amazing my God is. My injuries could have been much worse, but as it was, I received organic shrapnel from my teammates that removed my right eye and punctured my left eye, causing me to go blind instantly.

The explosion threw me to the ground and pinned me under my vehicle, breaking multiple bones and causing me to move in and out of consciousness. My skull was fractured in many places, as was my upper jaw. My Scottish nose had broken in eight places, and my beautiful face armor, that is, my beard, had been singed. My teammate Devin, who ran triage, was the first responder. He said that as he looked the team over, I started kicking my feet, which gave him the heads-up that I was still alive somehow. Thank you, restless leg syndrome. Even though I was covered in debris from the explosion, to the point that he swore I was dead, Devin helped me to my feet. While he attempted to get me to the road, where ambulances were lining up, I heard people yelling, "There is no way Turnbull is going to make it!" This was the first time I'd been given a 0 percent chance of survival. Challenge accepted. Not today, ISIS.

The ride from the explosion site to Furat Hospital was a quick one. I marveled the whole time at the luck of everything. Early in the deployment I had started doing assessments to figure out how I could help legitimize the local government. At this very moment, I was grateful that I had identified a shortfall in the medical system, in particular, the emergency transportation system. Just a few weeks earlier I had worked with the US Department of State to purchase and provide twenty ambulances for the local hospital. It was in one of these vehicles that I now was riding.

Once we arrived at the hospital, we were met by a young hospital administrator named Dr. Reem, a relationship with whom I had created by removing a land mine from a fridge in the basement of the hospital and burning ISIS propaganda that had been left hanging on the walls of the fourth floor. I again marveled, and blessed God, that we had identified the need for equipment and training for the hospital, which included the funding for a second operating room, provided by our great friend General Pond, and some items such as an ultrasound machine, which they were now using on my teammate Devin. Everything that other teammates had made fun of us for focusing on now brought a smile to my lips, knowing it was through my nonlethal aid that I had saved multiple members of my team and dozens of Syrians, with the bonus of increasing legitimacy for the local government while delegitimizing ISIS for their actions that day. This was what I called a very well-thought-out plan of action.

It was during this time that my boss, a.k.a. my hero, Colonel Jeff, happened to be flying overhead and heard of the attack. He went full Chuck Norris on the situation. Somehow there was a medical element in his helicopter, so he ordered the helicopter to land in the soccer field across the street from the hospital. When the pilot stated that they didn't have security, Colonel Jeff lifted his rifle and stated that he was their security, and they landed. This action marks Colonel Jeff as the greatest military leader of this time.

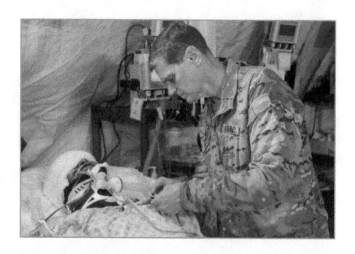

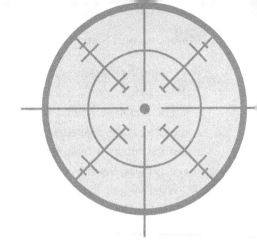

27

Back to Iraq and Germany

> Do not fear for I am with you; do not be dismayed
> for I am your God. I will strengthen you and help
> you; I will uphold you with my righteous hand.
>
> —Isaiah 41:10

I have been told by numerous people, including Colonel Jeff and his crew, that the events leading up to what happened after the explosion were very similar to certain scenes from the movie *Blackhawk Down*. Amid the chaos, Colonel Jeff's team was able to find Devin, Joe, and me, pull us from the hospital, and load us up in the medical evacuation (medevac) helicopter. We flew to another location in Syria, where they were not able to treat me, so another immediate medical evacuation was called for. During my second medevac, I stopped breathing and my heart stopped beating. Apparently, you need both things to stay alive. Rather than accept defeat and quit, a young man breathed for me via a handheld bag and performed CPR for around four hours, until we arrived in Iraq, at the US hospital in Baghdad.

The medevac landed in Baghdad. As the ramp was lowered, a medical team rushed up to the helicopter. The medical team unloaded my two teammates quickly. They were not in as bad a shape as I was, but they suffered from burns to their hands and faces. The chief of the ER, general surgeon Kyle, walked onto the bird and spoke with the flight surgeon. In a confident voice, the Baghdad surgeon asked, "Can you give me a rundown on this, soldier?"

The flight surgeon grunted through a partially closed mouth and replied with, "He died on the flight over. I give him zero percent chance of living another twenty-four hours."

Again? Challenge accepted.

I was taken off the bird. Kyle had a renewed vigor to ensure I would survive after the conversation with the flight surgeon. The first stop in the hospital was the room that contained a CT scanner. Kyle said that he sat in the room while I underwent the CT scan. As the pictures were being taken, I started thrashing around. Dr. Kyle got up and grasped my hand to calm me down. Toward the end of the scan, a nurse stormed into the room, demanding that Dr. Kyle come into the viewing room. Dr. Kyle later told me that he walked into the room and, seeing the nurses clustered around an image just taken, told everyone to get to work. Looking at the picture himself, he yelled, "Get Captain Turnbull prepped and into the operating room immediately. If we don't get that shrapnel out, there is zero percent chance that this guy is going to live!" As the surgeon gowned up, he rehearsed in his head the upcoming surgery that would determine if I lived or died.

Dr. Kyle cut my abdomen from my ribs to my groin so the team could remove my intestines, exposing two clusters of shrapnel. The first cluster was in my large intestine, which Dr. Kyle removed, along with a couple of inches of the intestine. The second cluster served as another clear demonstration that God was providing overwatch and protecting me, because a small piece of bone from one of my teammates was lodged in my iliac artery in my groin. According to the surgeon, such a thing was impossible because the pressure should have pushed the fragment out, or the jostling and moving from the past eight hours should have knocked it out. Either way, the bone should have popped out of the artery, which would have caused internal bleeding and would have caused me to die in less than five minutes. The only possible explanation for the bone's having lodged in the artery that the surgeon could think of was that God had his finger on it the entire time, from the explosion to the operating table. Dr. Kyle stated that he could not fabricate such a situation no matter how much duct tape, Gorilla Glue, or training he had had.

This dialogue between surgeons was relayed to the Turnbull family four months later at Walter Reed National Medical Center, when the general surgeon, Dr. Kyle, visited with me in my hospital room. He introduced himself to us and for some reason told us he was not a religious man. It was this simple wound that had made the surgeon state, "Because of what you went through, I know without a doubt there is a God. I also know that with him, I am now the best surgeon in the world, because there is no way on this earth that you should still be here."

Take that, ISIS.

After a day in Iraq, and after I'd received my Purple Heart from General Votel, I, Devin, and Joe were packaged up and loaded onto a military plane. The three of us were flown to Landstuhl Regional Medical Center (LRMC) in Germany. Upon our landing in Germany, the medical team ushered us soldiers from the airplane to the hospital. I remember that there was a real warm, comforting feeling alongside me during the move, which was vivid since this was in the heart of winter in Germany and I was void of clothes as I lay atop my hospital bed. The warm sensation had come from a man named Chaplain Nelson, who put a hand on my shoulder and leaned in close enough for me to hear him.

"Young man, you are safe and almost home. May the Lord bless you and keep you. May the Lord make his face shine upon you.

May the Lord give you peace. Amen." With that simple blessing, he squeezed my shoulder. Soon, I was in my room in the ER, surrounded by machines and nurses. For the next three days I was in and out of the ICU and the emergency department at LRMC in Germany. I had multiple surgeries to relieve the pressure from my brain, and my stomach was left open to help relieve the pressure there. I also had had my right eye removed, and they had started doing what they could to save my left eye. I was given medication to keep me under sedation so my body would start healing. Because my intercranial pressure (ICP) was so high, I was left in a dark room with no noise as often as possible.

Samantha and I quickly realized just how small this world we live in is. My dad is a corrections officer, and he had a boss whose daughter Holly lived within driving distance of the LRMC. She saw that Samantha had made a Facebook post asking for prayer. Holly had sent her a message just saying, "Ramstein/Landstuhl is a short trip for me if you need anything. Prayers for you and Ian as you wait." She had no idea what Sam's Facebook post meant, but she thought that it meant I was coming home since Samantha had told her a few days prior that I was supposed to be on my way back. She didn't think anything else about it simply because Sam was just asking for prayers, not having mentioned anything about me being hurt. Holly is a teacher, so she spent the rest of the afternoon in her classroom, although she had heard about the bombing in Syria. She knew I was there but figured that since Sam hadn't heard anything, I was just in a blackout zone while transitioning home. She was worried and not worried at the same time.

Holly went on her break. Having decided to go walk on the track, she started praying. For some reason, while she was praying for me, it swiftly changed to praying for the doctors, nurses, and other medical staff. She prayed for their wisdom, prayed for their hands, and prayed for perseverance. For thirty-plus minutes on the track, those were her prayers, even while thinking, *Why aren't I praying for the people injured?!*

Fast-forward to Thursday morning, Germany time. It was me. I was the one who had been hurt. More prayers went up from Holly. I was in Iraq at the time with the best trauma team in the world. Thursday night, I had been transported to Germany—Landstuhl. On Friday, January 18, Holly messaged her contact information to Samantha and my mom. People now were posting things on social media and emailing and calling my family left and right— news reporters, officers, military officials, JAG officers, et al. I can't imagine the stress my family faced, but Holly was what mattered to Sam now. Sam wanted Holly to go be with me while she couldn't be. Holly called the ICU and spoke with a captain who was extremely protective of me. I am very thankful for that. She explained how she knew me and Sam and explained why she was calling. The only thing the ICU told Holly was that I was stable, adding that if she were to come to the hospital, they could give her more information. Holly loaded up and drove over as quickly as she could after work on Friday.

Eventually, after finding out where I was, Holly discovered that she was not allowed back to see me, but my nurse Jennifer came out to talk with her. Holly didn't know my birthday, so she called Sam, who spoke to the nurses and gave them permission to speak to Holly. Of course, I was back in surgery to relieve the pressure on my brain at this point. Samantha was wanting more than anything to fly out to be with me. Still, the doctors and nurses were trying as hard as they could to get me to Walter Reed so my left eye could be saved. I would not be flying stateside until my ICP was stable and well below a ten. Because of the number of surgeries I needed to have, my ICP was around thirty. It had to be below twelve to be in a safe zone, so I had a long way to go. My nurse Jennifer told Holly that the plan was to fly me out on Saturday; however, it wasn't looking too promising. Holly messaged Sam and told her to get here as soon as possible.

On Saturday the nineteenth, Holly called in the morning to see if I could have visitors. The night before visitors were not permitted because of my high ICP. I was kept in a dark room, machines were silenced, and there were minimal nurse visits. Thankfully, with technology, they were monitoring my machines outside my room. This way I would have no stimulation. The nurse who had answered Holly's call was getting off his shift but said yes to visitors.

Holly drove over. The team introduced themselves to her. It was a blur of names, but people began to sort themselves out. Holly was sure they each had a specific job, but what mattered to her was that they were caring for me. The nurses apologized profusely for not having let Holly in the night before. She told them not to worry. Nurse Falco was my nurse that day. He was a very tall German civilian whom Holly referred to as "Mr. Clean." He, like the rest of the staff, was extremely protective of me. He would be the nurse who would trade shifts with Jennifer throughout my stay here at LRMC.

Nurse Falco talked with Holly while blocking the door to my room. He showed her how to put on a gown and gloves, because on top of everything else, I had tested positive on a panel screen. They had put me in quarantine of some sort to protect those in Germany from whatever might have been growing on or inside me from Syria. Holly came in with Falco and began talking with me. Falco told Holly she could touch me, so she found a spot on my left hand and forearm within her reach. She told me about walking the track and praying, and about my family loving me, where my parents were, how Ian was, what our new rabbits were up to, and their silly cowlicks. Eventually, Falco and another nurse left the room, at which point Holly began to talk to me about how she had lost her job and what her dream job would entail. She told me more about how loved I was and said that people were praying for me.

I loved that Holly was there, but I wanted my beautiful wife. Little did I know, after five long months, I was finally about to be reunited with the one person in my life who always made things better. Samantha was on her way to be with me. This would mark the end of my very last deployment.

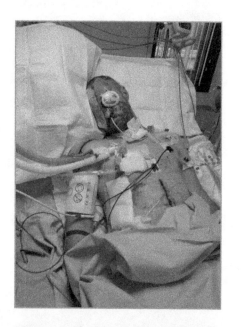

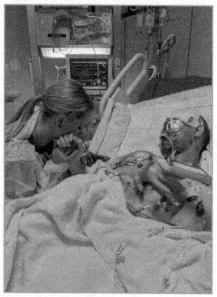

28

Sam's First Trip Overseas

May the Lord Bless you and keep you; may the Lord make
his face shine upon you and be gracious to you; may the
Lord turn his face toward you and give you peace.

—Numbers 6:24–26

The journey to get Sam to Germany is one I wish could have been
different. I wanted so badly to get home and take her on a trip since
she had never been overseas and hadn't been anywhere except the
East Coast of the United States. There is so much to see and do in
the world, and if there was anyone who deserved to see it, it was her.
Not only was she taking care of Ian, but also she was taking care of
two dogs, two rabbits, ten chickens, two ducks, the bills, chores, and
maintenance of our fourteen acres. On top of that, she managed the
homes we owned and had rented out and was preparing to welcome
me and Lambchop back home while remodeling our floors. I told
her I wanted to take her to Germany, Scotland, Ireland, and maybe
back to Jordan, then make a final stop in Israel. Five days before I

got hurt, she had gone to Walgreens to get her passport photo taken. Not having a passport made it hard for her to get to Germany, but thankfully the military worked it out to where she was able to make a stop at the State Department in DC and get one there before flying out. I am thankful that she can smile about her trip now.

Back home, Samantha was getting ready to head to Germany. Ian was extremely confused and scared at this point. Considering Samantha had only spent one night away from our son in six years, to attend a Josh Groban concert, he did not want her to leave. Ian cried and begged her not to go, fearing that she was going to get hurt as well. I don't know how she had thought about it quickly enough to tell Ian that, what with the two of them always having teased me by calling me Captain America, when any of the Avengers got hurt, they flew to Germany to be treated at the hospital that was treating me. Since I had lost my eye, Sam explained that she needed to help me find my way back, adding to Ian that the next time he saw her, I would be with her too. Ian asked Sam if I would be wearing an eye patch. After hearing I would be wearing an eye patch and then asking why, he said, "Well, since Daddy lost an eye, can we call him Thor now instead?!" The things that children say! I know, given my sense of humor, that God blessed us with a child just to make us laugh when we needed it most. That was the first time Samantha had laughed in days.

Samantha packed her bags and then packed Ian's bags. To provide our son with a distraction from life, my sister and aunt, who are the biggest Disney fans ever, decided to add Ian to their planned Disney cruise to the Bahamas. He would be going there with them in a few days. I am very thankful that Ian will forever have those memories. By now my parents, my sister, my nephew, and Sam's parents were now at our house in North Carolina, busy getting orders to travel and working with JAG to get the proper forms filled out with powers of attorney. Sam would be leaving in the morning, so she made sure to let our closest friends in North Carolina know what was going on and then asked for help with watching our animals and house. I am very thankful for the love and support we have in North Carolina and am forever grateful for everyone who helped us out.

The next morning, my in-laws took Sam to the airport with Ian. Sam kissed our son goodbye, not knowing when she would see him again. I know this feeling all too well. She met with Chaplain Jordan, and our unit surgeon, Jerry, at their gate, and soon they were all on their way to Reagan National Airport in DC. From there they would meet up with a driver named Mr. Steel, who would be taking them to the State Department to get Sam her passport. The fact that the State Department opened just for her, on a Sunday, says a lot about how much our government cares for our military families.

The process was quick and easy. With passport in hand, Sam called Mr. Steel to be picked up again. After getting a quick DC tour and trying to get Mr. Steel to say what his real name was, without any luck, they arrived at Dulles International Airport, where they were told to go directly to the USO and wait there until it was time to fly out. With their flight leaving at ten o'clock at night, and seeing that it was only three in the afternoon, they had quite a wait. Jordan signed them into the USO under his name, where they were able to pass some time by watching football. During the game, Sam got up and decided to call LRMC to get an update on me and let them know she was on her way there. While she was on the phone, the volunteers at the USO acted as if something was wrong, so Sam asked Jerry to go see what was going on. Since they had signed in under Jordan's name, they were worried Samantha had never made it to the USO. Come to find out, dinner reservations at the District Chophouse had been made for them and they were late to dinner.

They made their way to the restaurant. While looking over the menu, Sam was prepared to order a steak and a big filling dinner to last her for the eight-hour flight they were about to take since she hadn't eaten much the last four days. That was until she overheard Jerry and Jordan asking each other what vegetarian options were available. Sam laughed and said, "Wait. I'm going to Germany, a land filled with schnitzel, and neither of you eat meat?!" She was wanting to order the steak, but being polite, she met the guys halfway and ordered a club sandwich instead.

After finishing dinner, they were escorted back to the USO. Their escort tried to get them through security as quickly as possible and help them avoid the lines, but he failed miserably. They ended up walking about two miles through the airport instead. It was time for them to finally go to their gate, so, once arriving, Sam decided to call her parents and Ian before boarding, while Jerry read and Jordan watched the Rams defeat the Saints 26–23. With Sam on the phone, Jordan asked the flight attendant to upgrade Sam to the best seat available since their assigned seats were near the back of the plane. It was a gesture that Sam came to see as one of the many selfless acts of kindness Jordan performs.

As they boarded the plane, Sam was very happy to be going to be with me, yet at the same time she was very nervous, anxious, and scared. Sam knows without a doubt that Jordan was sent by God to help her through this trip. He came up to her seat just as anxiousness had taken over and asked if he could pray with her before they took off. The rest of the flight consisted of Sam trying to sleep without success and ended with Jordan praying again right before landing in Frankfurt.

Upon arriving, they wandered through customs, before meeting up with a liaison from the Care Coalition, named Chris. Chris would be taking care of Samantha, Jordan, and Jerry while they stayed at LRMC. From what I've been told, he was a no-nonsense army ranger who had the personality of a quiet, lethal man whom it was best not to mess with. He has gotten up one more time than he has been knocked down, and he has an inner drive to accomplish his missions. I found him to be intimidating, yet at the same time he had the biggest heart. He treated us as if we were a part of his family. Showing his concern, he wanted nothing but the best for us.

Sam, Jerry and Jordon got to Chris's vehicle. Sitting in the front seat, Sam noticed that the trees were flying past the car. This was her first trip on the Autobahn; she was afraid to ask how fast they were going. Upon arriving, Chris handed them each a phone to use while in Germany. These phones took them back to the late 1990s, early 2000s. Since we live in North Carolina, Samantha doesn't own a winter coat, so Chris pointed out that she was going to freeze, telling her that he would get her a coat to keep warm. He took her to the Fisher House, which would be her home away from home for the next few weeks. Having found out I was the only patient in the ICU, she realized that she would have the whole mansion to herself. Jordan told her to unload her luggage, get a shower, and meet them downstairs in an hour, at which time they would finally head over to see me.

It ended up being both the best day and the worst day for Samantha. I had a big morning of surgery, so when Samantha arrived at the hospital, she first ran into Holly and Chaplain Nelson. Chaplain Nelson prayed the same prayer over Samantha as he prayed over me, and Holly gave Samantha the hug that she had been needing for days. It was such a comfort for her to see a familiar face and be with someone who she knew would serve as the distraction she would need for the tough days ahead.

They all walked to the ICU waiting room, where they met Dr. Purtell, my lead trauma surgeon. She told Samantha to sit, then told her about my condition, stating that I had lost my right eye, I had no skin or tissue on the right side of my face, I had lost some of my teeth (or so they believed), I had multiple skull fractures, there were holes in my sides where shrapnel had entered, my stomach was completely open, my ribs were broken, and my hip was broken. Worst of all, my orbital socket had been shattered, the bone fragments having gone into my brain. The locations where these had entered were such that, more than likely, I would be paralyzed on my left side and would have a severe TBI (traumatic brain injury). More than likely, I would not remember much of anything, possibly including Samantha and our son. It would be a long road of recovery.

They told her that I would never be the husband she remembered and that I would never be the man I used to be. She told Sam that before she went in, they would make sure to have a chair behind her because she would more than likely pass out. If that weren't enough, Dr. Purtell then told my wife what surgeries had already taken place and what would be happening in the next few weeks. Worst of all was when she said, "Please do not get your hopes up. He is stable for now, but we don't expect much improvement. And if he does improve, it is going to be a miracle."

Samantha then began the walk of her life. She and I were finally about to be reunited, but this was not the reunion either of us had planned for. Samantha wanted very badly to run into my arms and hug me, but she knew this would not happen. Every spouse longs for the first embrace after a deployment, so for her to have to see me like this, she knew, was the hardest thing in the world to do. She was given a yellow gown and gloves to put on. While putting them on, she saw me through a crack in the curtains. Her heart skipped a few beats at the sight of me, but then she rounded the corner of my door and, in that moment, had every type of emotion run through her. She was both happy to see that I was alive and broken to see how lifeless I was. She has said that if it weren't for the fact that she could see my heart beating, she wouldn't have thought I was alive. My ventilator kept inflating my chest, then deflating it, and I was completely absent of movement. I was cold, and my body was so swollen, she said, that it looked as if I were made of plastic. She did everything she could to keep from crying in front of everyone, but the tears fell anyway. She didn't pass out, thankfully. Instead, because of what she was seeing, a smile came to her face. She had been told she wouldn't recognize me, but from what she could see of my face, which was my lips and chin—my head was otherwise completely wrapped in bandages—she did recognize that part of me. That was why she was smiling. She was also kind of glad that the beard I had grown out during the deployment had mostly been singed off, so it looked in a way as if I had shaved. No matter how bad I looked, Samantha was very happy to be with me. She spent the rest of the day beside me, holding my hand, talking to me, and praying.

It was time for her to leave because doctors said my ICP was up again, so she kissed my hand and told me how thankful she was to have been given this second chance, along with the opportunity to tell me just one more time that she loved me. After having spent the past five days with very little sleep, traveling, worrying, and waiting to see me again, Sam was happy to be just across the street now. Still, leaving my room was the hardest thing she had ever had to do. She asked Jordan and Jerry to go with her to get something to eat from the cafe.

They laughed when they got there. Remember the conversation where Samantha told Ian that the Avengers go to LRMC? Well, as she, Jerry, and Jordan were getting ready to pay for the dinner they'd just eaten, they saw a huge banner above the cash register that had "LRMC" printed on it. Within the lines of each letter, a different Marvel character was depicted. The banner made Sam realize at that moment that life was going to be all right. Silly things like this were about to start showing up frequently. It was nice for me to find out later that she had started laughing again.

Jordan and Jerry walked her back to Fisher House, telling her where they were staying and saying that they were just a phone call away if she needed anything. Jordan told her they would be going to the gym at five in the morning; if she wanted to join them, she was more than welcome. She laughed, telling them her world didn't start revolving until at least seven, adding that they should have fun. Since they would be up for the shift change, during which time Jerry could listen to any reports and learn about any medical changes, they would call her with any updates, they said. She went up to her room, took a shower, and called home, and was able to speak with Ian briefly before she crashed. She knew God was going to take care of everything. With her faith, she knew I was going to make it. She closed her eyes and slept the best she had ever slept, being at peace in the knowledge that only God provides.

29

Marvelous Miracles

Your workmanship is marvelous—how well I know it.

—Psalm 139:14

I ended up staying in Germany for three weeks. From what I have been told, while I was there, many things happened for which there was no explanation, or sometimes there was 0 percent chance that x, y, or z—something related to my recovery—could have happened as it had. This "0 percent chance" has become the motto of my life and the foundation of my faith, because when there is 0 percent chance of something happening, it only means that it is 100 percent God-driven when the very thing thought to be impossible does happen. So, I don't mind when there is a 0 percent chance, because at these times I know that great unexplained things are about to happen.

One morning after Samantha had come up to my room, the doctors told her that overnight they had made the decision that they would be prepping for surgery that afternoon to amputate the index finger of my right hand. The tip of my finger had started to turn a dark blue, which had spread down to my second knuckle. The finger was not getting circulation. Ultrasounds were taken, and sure enough, no pulse was found in the finger. Samantha called Jerry instantly to come to my room. Knowing how much I loved being out at our gun range, she said to the doctors, once Jerry had arrived, "We *have* to save Jon's finger! It is his trigger finger! There must be something we can do. His finger just needs to be moved or something!" I am very glad she is the type of wife who knows more about me than I know about myself, and also that she doesn't back down from a fight. While holding my hand, she felt how cold it was and said she wanted to start moving my hands, arms, feet, and legs, as long as it was allowed. Then she asked Jerry if he thought a heat pack would help bring circulation back to the finger. He agreed it was a great idea. Even though the doctors were hesitant and unsure it would work, they agreed to give it a try, with the caveat that if there was no improvement within two hours, they would perform the surgery.

Chaplain Jordan and Nelson came in and prayed. Heat was applied to my finger, and within an hour, the color had returned. Surgery was canceled. My trigger finger / safety finger was saved! Praise God for surrounding me with the right people and giving them the ability to save me!

Samantha had gotten permission from the doctors to start moving my limbs for me, which she was doing to keep my body from getting stiff. The thought of having a blind, paralyzed husband was almost too much for her to bear. She would spend her time in my room making sure to move my left side. Doctors would take me off sedation and would come in and pinch my chest on the left to try to get any reaction from me. I wouldn't move my left side at all, instead only reaching with my right hand to stop them from pinching me. I was on heavy drugs that made me sleep for the greater part of each day. The times when I came off sedation were some of Sam's favorite parts of the day. The first time I was coming off sedation, the doctors wanted to see how much of my brain was still working, so they asked Sam to be there to talk to me. While I was coming to consciousness, she simply said, "Jon, it's me, Sam. You don't have to do anything. I

just want you to know that I am here with you and that I love you."
She started crying when I squeezed her hand three times. The nurses
were confused as they hadn't seen any reaction from me, so Sam
explained that whenever we couldn't say "I love you" to each other
out loud, we had always squeezed our hands together three times to
replace the words. Sam was happy that I knew who she was. In that
moment, nothing else mattered.

This is another example of God's work. The doctors had said I
had 0 percent chance of remembering anything or moving my left
side ever again because of the bone fragments that had lodged in
my brain, yet that 0 percent turned into 100 percent with God in
charge. This is what I realized once I regained consciousness and
remembered that Samantha was my wife.

So, there I was. It was a new day. The staff told Sam that
new doctors were going to be doing an ultrasound of my left eye.
Samantha, telling them that she was a dental assistant, got permission
to clean my teeth. As I drifted in and out of consciousness, I knew
my wife was present, this episode being the first thing I remember
of my wife after I'd awakened.

I awoke to someone with a hand in my mouth, feeling along my
teeth. It was a very weird experience. Sam was pleasantly surprised
that I still had all my teeth. As the team came in to conduct the
ultrasound, they noted that Sam was dressed appropriately for their
procedure, so they asked if she would assist in the ultrasound. Since
she had practiced keeping her hand steady as a dental assistant, she
was given an ultraviolet light to shine so the team could examine
my remaining eye. As they dropped medicine in my eye, the light
would indicate any living tissue. As Sam held the light over my eye,
she knew for sure that I was blind because nothing in my eye lit up.
Instead of seeing a blue eye, she gazed up something that looked
like a gray-colored raisin. The doctors commented to her that they
didn't have to tell her the outcome or results because she had seen for
herself, adding that there was more than likely 0 percent chance that
I would ever have vision in my left eye again. They told her that they

were keeping up their hopes for saving my eye, adding that they had contacted my ophthalmologist at Walter Reed. They had FaceTimed with this doctor and conducted another ultrasound while Samantha had held the phone. The main point of this ultrasound was to see what kind of time span they were looking at before getting me back home stateside. They needed to get me to Walter Reed as soon as possible to save my left eye. During the ultrasound FaceTime, Marcus, Walter Reed ophthalmologist, saw that there was a large blood clot inside my eyeball. The blood clot would not liquefy for at least ten days, according to him, which gave the doctors at LRMC that much time to get my ICP down so I could be transported back home. Sam called my folks and told them we would be at LRMC for at least ten more days, so if they wanted to come, now was the time to do so. That was the moment they decided to come to Germany and be with their baby (barrel-chested freedom fighter with face armor) boy.

While this was going on, Samantha noticed that she hadn't gotten the ophthalmologist's name. She said that she needed his name just in case she had any questions. The nurse commented that he had heard Samantha talking about the Avengers and had decided not to tell her his name because he was embarrassed by the coincidence. Being a civil affairs spouse who was used to my negotiation tactics, Sam convinced the doctor to tell her his name. Of course, my doctor at LRMC would be Steve Rogers, adding yet another layer to our son's belief that the Avengers always went to LRMC when they needed medical care.

The rest of the time I spent in Germany consisted of surgeries and wound clean-outs. Thankfully, at the time I was the only patient in the ICU, which meant I had the best care possible without any distractions. Samantha was extremely well taken care of and, thanks to Holly, took some time to get outside the hospital a little bit too. Her family is from Germany. It was wonderful to know that she was able to get a little taste of where she came from.

When my parents arrived, Sam was very glad to have them there to help her out. Having a son of my own, I cannot imagine how hard it was for my parents to see me the way I was. It was comforting to have them there with me, along with Sam. I know without a doubt that without the support of my family, my recovery wouldn't have been the same. I know that if I had been alone without anyone else, I may have decided not to fight to stay alive. I thank my parents and my wife for sticking with me, being beside me, and helping me fight.

Now comes the fun part. While sitting beside my bed massaging my feet and hands, Sam was thinking about why my body wasn't moving on the left side. For some reason, she kept telling herself, *It's just muscle memory. Jon has to use his muscles, or he is going to lose his ability to move.* My body was still extremely heavy from the fluids and swelling. Sam worked on moving my fingers one at a time, then moved on to opening and closing my fist, after that working my wrists and arms. From there she would perform much the same routine with my toes, ankles, and knees. She was exhausted but figured she might as well help me in any way she could.

One afternoon, a nurse walked in and asked Sam why she was doing this. Sam simply stated, "I'm not giving up on my husband. He will move his left side again one day." The nurse said he thought it was nice of her to do what she doing, and she asked if I could be taken off sedation for a little while so she could talk with me. The small team of medical people started waking me up, and Sam started talking, even though she knew I couldn't reply. She said, "Jon, can you do me a favor and give me a thumbs-up with your left hand? I want you to prove these people wrong. I know you aren't paralyzed." Being the husband that I am, I didn't want to upset her or let her down. With the nurse watching, I gave a thumbs-up with my left hand. Sam, of course, started crying, and the nurse ran out of the room screaming. It was one of the happiest moments for Sam. They decided to start weaning me off sedation as much as possible, and I began to improve a little more each day.

The more that fluid left my body, the more I began to move. The fact that I could move again soon became a blessing and a curse according to everyone involved. I began touching most of my wounds, trying to figure out what had happened to me, and I didn't like not being able to talk to anyone because of the trach I had in. I started writing on paper, saying that I wanted a shower or something to drink, and asking Sam why she was in the room with me. Not fully being aware of what was going on, and being heavily medicated, I would scare Sam sometimes. She remembers that I had asked if it was Victory Over Japan Day, and once I even told her I needed to save the POWs in the hospital. I was, in my mind, still in Syria, so I was terrified to know the reason she was with me. I told her multiple times that she had to leave and that she wasn't safe. Thankfully she didn't leave, the nurses having described hospital delirium to her.

Samantha hated that I couldn't talk and knew I must have been bored out of my mind. My ICP was still high. Talking with Chaplain Jordan, she asked him if he would go get a nurse. Falco was on the shift this day. Sam told him that before the explosion, whenever I wanted to relax at home, I would either have the television on or be listening to music. Unlike my wife, I find that noise makes me more comfortable, and I hate being bored. Sam asked Falco if it would be okay if she and Jordan turned some music on in my room. Saying that he didn't think that it would be allowed, he told her that he would ask the doctors anyway. Sam asked him to tell the doctors that if the music contributed to a rise in my ICP in any way, she and Jordan would turn it off.

Thankfully, the doctors agreed to give it a try. Jordan asked Sam what type of music I liked. He used his Spotify to turn on Casting Crowns. Another miracle happened just then. Almost instantly, my ICP went from the twenties down to around twelve. The music was kept on for the rest of my stay at LRMC. Falco said he had never heard of Casting Crowns before but that he really liked the music. The next day, when Sam and Jordan came up, Falco was on shift again, but this time he had Casting Crowns playing on the phone in his back pocket. With smiles on their faces, Sam and Jordan couldn't help but laugh seeing him work with a little spring in his step, a side of him they had never expected to see. What made them laugh, though, was that when he bent over to get some medical supplies, they noticed his phone had a PopSocket on the back, and the PopSocket was the Captain America shield.

Three weeks after my arrival in Germany, my ICP finally dropped to ten. The doctors determined it was time to let me go home. In three days, I would be on my way back to the United States.

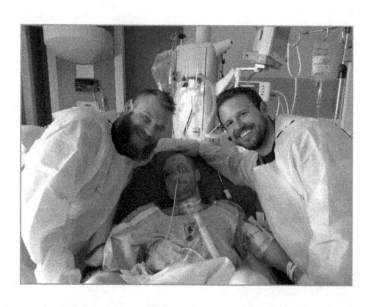

30

Going Home

Go home to your friends and tell them how much the Lord has done for you and how much he has had mercy on you.

—Mark 5:19

My family, Chaplain Jordan, Doc Jerry, and I were packed and ready to go. I was wheeled out of the hospital in one of the smaller hospital beds and was loaded into a school bus with half its back seats removed so hospital beds could be wheeled into it for transport. The bus was basically a large ambulance. Leaving Landstuhl, we drove to Ramstein Air Base, where a C-17 was waiting for us. After I was put on the airplane, Chaplain Nelson said goodbye to us in the same manner he had said hello to us when we arrived. With everyone huddled around my gurney, he prayed for us all. With tears in his eyes, he blessed us on our journey by saying, "May the Lord bless you and keep you. May his face shine upon you." What an incredible human being. I will forever be thankful for this man and his prayers and faithfulness.

We had to wait a bit to take off, but once we were in the air, we were on our way home. As silly as this may sound, for the first time in the fifteen years that my wife and I had been together, this was our very first plane ride together.

The trip took much longer than usual because of another miracle. The pilots had overheard the doctors say that they wouldn't let me leave just yet because they feared my ICP would spike again if the plane were to fly higher than ten thousand feet. Another spike, they said, could be life-threatening. The pilots were the ones who had interjected on my behalf, so they agreed to fly the aircraft lower than five thousand feet for the entire tripe! At that altitude, my family would surely freeze on the flight.

We took off and were told to expect a long flight back. My mom ended up taking many trips to the bathroom just to stay warm. Thankfully, C-17's are big enough to allow you to get up, walk around, and stretch. Sam and my mom were amazed when they looked out the small window of the aircraft and saw the whitecaps of the waves below them.

Ten or so hours later, at around ten thirty in the evening, we touched down in Washington, DC. I was finally back home thanks to those incredible air force pilots. Gentlemen, I do not know you, but I cannot thank you enough for everything you did that day. For that I will proudly say, "Go, Air Force football, beat Navy!"

Upon arriving at Andrews Air Force Base (now Joint Base Andrews), we were greeted by groups of civilians and soldiers. My family was happy to be getting the chance to see Air Force One up close—a cool sight to see after what they had witnessed over the last few weeks. I was put on a small school bus / ambulance that would drive us the hour's distance to Walter Reed. Arriving at Walter Reed, we were greeted by my boss, my very dear friend Master Sergeant Jamie, and a woman who became our angel during my recovery, Heidi, our new liaison from the Care Coalition. Little did we know that she would quickly become more than just a liaison; she was soon to be one of our lifelong friends.

I was immediately taken to the ICU. As soon as I was wheeled into the room, my ophthalmologist, Dr. Marcus, was there to start working on my left eye. An ultrasound was done. I would be going into surgery first thing in the morning. Samantha had to fill out a lot of paperwork. While I was getting settled in, she was told she and my parents needed to leave to go check in to the hotel where they would be staying for the remainder of my time here, however long that may be. Samantha had never felt this exhausted in her life. She checked into her hotel room and tried as hard as she could to sleep, even though it seemed impossible with so many changes taking place. Whether she was just tired and nervous or simply full of emotion, she ended up passing out in the bathroom. After coming to, she grabbed a snack to eat, just in case it was low blood sugar making her sick, then drank some water and went to bed. I know without a doubt that Samantha had passed out because the reality had finally sunk in that life would never be the same again.

The next morning, Sam met with my boss, Jamie, Chaplain Jordan, and Doc Jerry, and said farewell to each of them. She was sad and a little overwhelmed by their departure because it meant that for the first time, she and my parents would have no support other than Heidi. After getting lost and walking a mile in the hospital, Sam found her way to my room in the ICU, arriving just before I was wheeled out for surgery. I was going to be getting a cornea transplant, and the doctors were going to perform exploratory surgery to determine if my left eye could be saved. The corneal transplant surgery was expected to take around five hours. Whereas this part of the surgery was a success, unfortunately, the overall surgery was not successful. Three hours into the procedure, Dr. Marcus came into the waiting room with a look of defeat on his face. He informed Sam and my parents that the retina had detached from my left eye, which had folded in half on itself. My optic nerve was sliced. The fluid inside my eyeball was leaking out, causing the whole system of vision in my left eye to shut down. For the third time, doctors were telling them that they had tried everything they could to save my eye, but there was 0 chance I would ever see again. Samantha was tired of hearing bad news. Unable to take any more heartache, she began to pray harder than she ever had before. At every opportunity, she would post updates on Facebook asking for specific prayers each day. From that moment on, God began showing up and proving that faith, over medicine, was the best option. And "hand of God" moments began happening.

Two days into my stay at the ICU, my occupational therapists came into my room and told me it was time for me to get up and moving. With my family and a few close friends around, I very weakly stood for the first time. What a joy to be able to stand and get out of bed. So much for being paralyzed. I was then put into a chair. Heidi entered my room with a small whiteboard for me to start writing on so I could communicate better. Since I had my trach in, I could not talk, and I was going through a lot of paper. A whiteboard sure helped save some trees. And Sam learned she could quickly erase things that would be embarrassing to have others see. I was also going to be starting TBI assessments to determine the extent of my head injury. Since my right eye socket had been pushed back into my brain, I was tested again to see how much I could remember. With the whiteboard in hand, I began drawing a tank upside down and backward, showing that I was dreaming of a tank with an oil leak. After that I was asked if I had any questions about what was going on. In reply, I wrote the first thing that came to mind. While writing upside down and backward, I asked, "Where is Lambchop?" Samantha told me he was being taken care of and was getting ready to be shipped to Fort Bragg, where one of my best friends would be picking him up. Then she asked me if there was anything else I wanted to ask. Being a loving husband, and knowing that I would cause her extreme embarrassment, I took the opportunity to break the ice and let my humor shine. With the doctors, the nurses, some friends, and my dad standing beside me, I simply wrote, "Can we have sex?" My dad read it out loud and burst into laughter. I couldn't see my wife, but I just knew her face was beet red. I hated not being able to speak so I could let everyone know I was doing okay. Being blind and mute was miserable. I am very thankful that at least I was able to write my thoughts down.

Within the first week of being at Walter Reed, I was lucky to be going to the bathroom nonstop. Thanks to the water in Syria, I tested positive for *E. coli*. The fact that I was still going to the bathroom, as well as throwing up constantly, meant that Sam and the nursing staff had to change my sheets about every twenty minutes. I was very embarrassed. It occurred to Samantha that I might have the flu. The nurse said that this was impossible because I had gotten a flu shot before I deployed and had been given another one as a precaution upon arriving in Germany. Sam asked that I be tested just in case. A few hours later, Sam was told to make sure she was wearing a mask when around me, and if she started feeling sick in any way, to go to the ER. Within an hour, I had tested positive for type A influenza. I bless God for ensuring that Sam has been by my side throughout this journey. Another useful thing she did was when she looked at the food I was being fed and told the nurses that because I was lactose-intolerant, I needed different food. From the moment they started feeding me as Sam asked, my health started improving tremendously. I was released to go down to an inpatient ward on the fourth floor. My stay here would be some of the best and some of the worst times of my life. So many memories were about to be made. The care I received on 4 Center was the best care I could ever have asked for.

Another angel who was involved with me at this time was one of my best friends and teammates, Shane. Shane was formerly a soldier with whom I had deployed a few years back. Upon hearing of the attack, he got involved, contacting Samantha and telling her that he would be available at any time. When I got to DC, he was also there, on assignment for the Department of State. Shane came to Walter Reed to help me and Samantha. It was at a time when I was refusing to take a shower. For some reason, the water in my room was freezing cold, so I was doing anything I could to avoid taking a shower. When Shane showed up, using his loud bass voice, he shouted to

Samantha, "What can I do to help you guys out?" Samantha said that I needed a shower, and he told everyone in the room, "I used to work in an assisted-living home. I can make Jonno take a shower." With that announcement, Shane got me out of bed and threatened me. I took the shower and got my payback by sloshing water, soap, and my filth onto his Doc Marten shoes. He told me that he would hold this event over my head for the rest of my life, but thanks to friends like Shane, it would be a much longer life, since he is the one who prevented me from dying of stink in my hospital bed.

Although I thanked Shane for helping me shower, I did not plan on taking another one. Walter Reed had a habit that added to my defiance in the face of showering: they placed their baby wipes in ovens to heat them to a comfortable temperature. These warm baby wipes were life-changing in that never again would I use a cold one. Next to the baby wipes, the nurses had placed the hospital blankets in the same heaters. Since it was winter and the hospital was kept at subzero temperatures, I requested blankets often. One morning Samantha came into my room and was barely able to see me under the approximately twenty blankets on top of me. My nurse, feeling sorry for me, had grabbed me a blanket every time I asked for another one. I remember the event well because that heap of blankets kept the cold away, although the weight almost smothered me.

My buddy Shane not only was a cruel, freezing-cold-shower slave driver, but also he got a few good laughs in. When my breathing tube was finally taken out, I again refused to do what the nurses asked of me, which this time was that I talk. Sam did what she could, but the meds I was on made me extremely stubborn and sometimes mean. Sam got upset and decided it was time to call the only person she knew who could help: Shane. All she had to say to him was, "Shane, I need your help." Luckily for her, he was currently walking down the hallway.

Sitting to my left, Shane talked to me in his indirect, forceful voice: "Jon, you are going to speak, brother. I promised Samantha that I would get you to say something. Jon, now is the time. You are going to tell Sam that you love her." I sat there quietly, knowing that my silence was annoying Shane. I wanted to see what he would do. He shook his head and stood over me with a hand on my left shoulder. "Jon, tell Sam that you love her!" He repeated this three times until he was at the point of yelling. I knew that my outright refusal to speak was leaving the realm of funny and becoming inappropriate or disrespectful. I knew I had to give it a try. After all, hadn't they told me that I had 0 percent chance of speaking for a few months after having my breathing tube removed?

I nodded in acknowledgment of Shane's words and opened my mouth to try to speak. I had been refusing to speak because when I tried, I sounded like a robot, and I was afraid to hurt the hole in my neck. Also, I had a lot of fluid in my chest and face, and when I was speaking, this fluid moved around, causing me to cough violently.

I whispered a quick prayer to God, asking for his help in speaking. I mouthed the words Shane had asked me to speak, but little sound came out.

Now was the time. I prayed harder because I wanted to prove the doctors had been wrong in giving me 0 percent chance of speaking. I wanted to show them how awesome my God is, and I also didn't want to let Shane down. I have the utmost respect for this man, and I wanted to make him proud of me. I also liked being funny, so after Shane instructed yet another time, "Jon, you can do it. Tell Samantha that you love her," I opened my mouth and, with all my being, shouted, "I love Shane!" The room fell silent, and I had the largest smile on my face.

I sensed that Shane was shaking his head as he blurted out, "Jon, No!" While chuckling, he got the words out, "Jon, tell *Samantha* that you love her. Do it right this time!" I nodded again, feeling content that I had made him laugh.

Opening my mouth once again, I said, "I love all Shanes?"

Shane slapped my shoulder and told me that I needed to be appropriate; I was embarrassing Samantha in front of the nurses. I love bringing humor to the room, but Shane was right. After hearing him again say, "Jon, tell Samantha that you love her. She is your everything, and she deserves to hear that from you," I was able to whisper, "I love Samantha." I could speak, even if I was saying things that were inappropriate. It was all a win. In case you are wondering, I did end up talking more to Samantha. I asked her to pick me up a doughnut. I was starving!

Shane was able to do one last incredible thing for me. It was time for me to get out of the ICU and onto the floor where I knew I had been healed much quicker than I should have. This was on the 4 Center ward, and 4 Center would now and forever be my Walter Reed home. I still think fondly of the place. Sergeant First Class Timmy B came walking down the hall, wheeling my IV pole with a drip bag of medicine attached. We laughed, saying that Timmy B was my street-corner pharmacist. Shane asked Timmy B, "Who put you in charge of Jon's medicine?"

Timmy B didn't skip a beat: "No one, but I'm a medic and can handle it!" Meanwhile, Samantha had gone down and gotten lunch, not knowing this was happening. On the way back to the ICU, she saw Shane's smile a mile away as he was helping to push my bed down the hallway. She couldn't believe what was happening. They got me settled into my new room; that's what mattered.

Shane and Timmy B are two amazing friends who would help me through a lot over the next eighteen months. But I would be failing to mention some important person if I didn't talk about my former company commander Ryan, whom we called "Slaw-Dawg," who came to my rescue on many occasions. He was often in my room. I appreciated his friendship. I thanked him one day for having driven five hours to visit with me when he had much more important things to deal with. He let me know that he had come up to see our former battalion commander, so the purpose of his trip was not exclusively to see me. That stung, sir.

I got Slaw-Dawg back one day when he asked how I was. I told him that I was happy. General Milley, the chairman of the Joint Chiefs of Staff, had come into my room earlier. When I had asked to be promoted, he took the Velcro patch indicating the rank of major that I was holding in my hand. The patch had come from Major Nick, who at the time was my executive officer, along with being a respected friend, but General Milley is the one to have put it on my uniform, which I had hanging up in the closet. I asked him for the paperwork frocking me to major, but instead of that, he gave me his business card, saying that if anyone needed to be corrected, I should have them call him direct. After telling this to Ryan, I added, "He also did something else." General Milley's wife had made me some chocolate chip cookies and brought them to me. I asked Sam to hand each of us one of Mrs. Milley's cookies. While we were eating our cookies, I told Slaw-Dawg what my goals were. "So, technically now I am a major."

Ryan nodded and, being in between bites, spit a few cookie crumbs out while speaking: "Not really, Jon! We have to talk about this because there is a lot more to it."

I heard this but still decided to try to be the funny guy I normally am. "Next, I am supposed to meet with the president. He has the ability to promote me too." Ryan said this was true. I continued: "I will ask for another promotion, from major to lieutenant colonel, and then I am going back home. And I'll fire Major Slaw-Dawg!" I chuckled to myself, knowing that he was right next to me and that everyone would think that, rather than being funny, I was acting this way because I was drugged.

Ryan had heard me loud and clear. Standing up, he shouted, "Jon, you are not nice." I felt bad, but the joke was still pretty funny to me. One day I want to be more like my former boss Major Ryan. He took the time out of his busy schedule to stop by and see me, and that meant the world.

Many friends and family members from all over the world came to visit me. I bless God for the friends I have made throughout my military career. Without the visits, I would have gone insane or given up on everything, I'm sure. I wish that for some visits I had been awake and not so drugged up, as then I could have had more laughs and reminisced about the good old days. I apologize for any visits where I wasn't totally there, but everyone who visited me should know that their visits meant the world not only to me, but also to my wife and family.

My only focus in life now was to do everything I could to get out of the hospital.

31

Hadassah

I will not cause pain without allowing
something to be born, says the Lord.

—Isaiah 66:9

It is amazing what the brain does. I remember conversations that I had with Samantha during my recovery; however, I was not awake during them. For example, I was in an apartment overlooking a harbor. Samantha was in the living room talking to me as I prepared supper in the kitchen. I was telling her that I loved her very much and that I was excited to marry her one day. She told me that we were married. I remember the feeling of shock and confusion at her answer. She then handed me an envelope, which I promptly opened while watching a boat park along the docks below. Inside the envelope were two pictures. The first was of a young boy with blond hair and very blue eyes. It was a picture of me, but when I was seven years old. Samantha stated that it was a picture of a boy named Ian and that he was our seven-year-old boy. He was living with my parents while I was being fixed at the hospital. The second picture was different. I wouldn't know who it was for a couple of months.

A couple of months later I was at Walter Reed National Medical Center and another miracle occurred. While on the fourth ward in room 427, I slept very little. My schedule was simple: At 2000 hours, everyone left for the night and I tried to sleep. At 0600, Samantha would come up to my room with breakfast before I got a couple of shots.

One night in my room, something angelic occurred. I had just fallen asleep when a very dark presence came into my room. It told me that God hated me, that this is why I had lost my vision, and that I would never see again. The adversary deepened my depression by telling me that I would never see my son graduate or ever see my wife again. It was a very hard night. I felt myself slipping into madness when I said a quick prayer for help. I shut my eyes and slipped into unconsciousness.

A few hours later, I awoke, startled by another presence in my room. This one was different from the evil one that had been present earlier. Hearing a young woman humming, I turned my head to see a young girl between me and my door smiling and humming. This little girl had curly raven-black shoulder-length hair and wore a blue and white horizontally striped sundress. Noticing that I had seen her, she smiled and lifted a petite hand to wave at me. She skipped over to my bed and asked in the sweetest voice, "How are you doing?" Everything about her indicated calm confidence and peace. I spoke to her for a few short moments about the depressing individual who was in the room, and she calmed me down before I fell back asleep.

The next morning after Samantha brought up breakfast, I spoke to the nurse, asking her, "Was there a little girl walking around the ward last night?"

My nurse looked at me, speechless, and walked over to my bed, placing a hand on my forehead. "Are you feeling okay, Captain Turnbull?"

Samantha, grabbing my hand after the nurse had left my room, said, "Jon, I think that girl may have been an angel sent here to help you. If you see her again, ask her."

The very next night I was awakened again in the same way, except this time the little girl was sitting on a couch to my left, kicking her feet while singing to herself. "Excuse me, young lady," I whispered. "Are you an angel?"

She looked at me with a grin on her face. "Jon, I am what I am, and I am here to help you." I then asked her if she had the ability to speak to God, and she replied that she spoke with him often.

"Can you ask God something for me? Why does he allow bad things to happen to people who love him, like me?"

She nodded while I spoke and then continued to hum. I lay there listening to her, when she suddenly stopped and said, "God wants you to know that he allows things like this to happen only to those he knows can handle them, such as you. Additionally, he allows bad things to happen to good people because it shows them he loves them."

In an attempt at humor, I rebutted, "Can you ask God to love me less?"

She shook her head no. Around 0600, I turned to my angel and told her, "You are welcome to stay here forever, but my wife, Samantha, is going to be here soon with breakfast, and she sits there where you are sitting."

The little girl smiled a very big smile, and then said, "By Samantha, you mean my mom?" My heart stopped at that moment, as did all thought.

Backtrack to four months before I deployed to Syria. Samantha had had a miscarriage; we believed the child was going to be a daughter. After I relayed this encounter to Samantha and my father, who was present this day, we all concluded that we believe that God sent Hadassah, my and Sam's baby girl who passed away, to protect me from the evil one when I was most vulnerable.

Hadassah, I love you, my baby girl. I cannot wait to meet you in heaven and share a hamburger with you!

32

Scars

He heals the brokenhearted and bandages their wounds.

—Psalm 147:3

"What is this?" I cringe at this question every time my wife asks it of me. Figuring that Sam was looking at something, I was grateful to know that my phone had been lost in the explosion, so I wouldn't have to explain any of the pictures on it that might be associated with missions that we might have done that I had taken to cover myself. Just a few days ago I had had my trach removed after I had fought with it, trying to pull it out myself, even on the verge of tearing the stitch that was keeping it in place. I did not like it being shoved down my throat; it was constantly choking me. After that choking device was removed, I pulled the feeding tube out of my nose. That was gross because along with it came a lot of boogers, plus mucus and blood. I had some of my closest friends from my unit in the room with me, and the nurses started to fight me as I started to remove these devices. I had already removed my IV, so I was on the verge of being better. As the nurses ran to stop me from harming myself further, I pulled the last thing out of my body: my catheter. With them yelling at me to stop, I just started to spin it around, flinging urine all over the place. That kept them away from me and got me laughing.

Samantha, at this point, was exhausted, constantly on her feet, making sure I wasn't pulling any more things out of my body. Knowing how important it was to keep my IVs in, she didn't want me hurting myself anymore. She was tired of having to yell at me as if I were mostly a four-year-old. With the frustrations of doctors constantly changing plans and bringing her bad news, with all the family drama, and with the simple wish that life would be completely different, she questioned what was going on in life daily and was in constant prayer. To be honest, she was beginning to doubt her faith and question whether God was still on her side. In that moment, as she held my left hand in both her hands, she looked out my window and simply prayed, "God, where are you?"

That is when I heard her ask me again, "What is this?!" Her fingers were tracing something on the back side of my left hand. As a reminder, Devin and Joe had been badly burnt from the explosion. Somehow, I hadn't been burned at all, but as Samantha held my hand, she told me that I had a very tiny burn on my hand. It was in the perfect shape of a cross and was bright pink in color. She saw it as a sign that God had protected me during the explosion. This potentially minor thing led two very close family members to get the same image tattooed on the same spot on their hands.

The image showed us that God continues to work in amazing ways and that no matter how bad things may seem, he is there as a shelter for those who ask. To this day, this cross shape in my flesh is one of the only nonsurgical scars I have left on my body. And it is one I am thankful for. Whenever I feel it or it is brought up, it reminds me of a song sung by one of my favorite bands, I Am They, called "Scars." Without the scars I have, I can say that I wouldn't know how amazing God is. So, I am thankful for these scars.

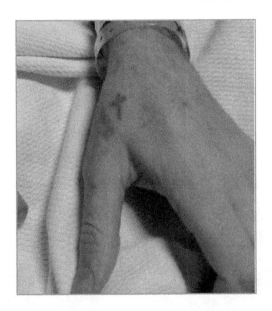

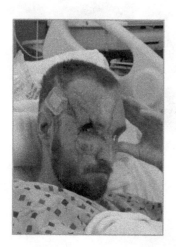
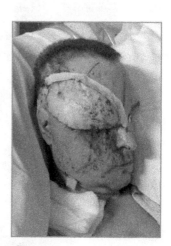

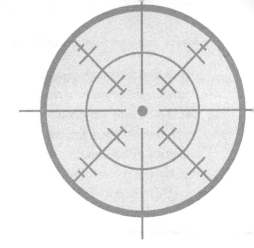

33

Dr. Dre

It is not those who are healthy who need a
physician, but those who are sick.

—Matthew 9:12

Not only was I needing surgery on my left eye, but also I was needing surgery where my right eye once was. My doctor was an incredibly smart man, someone I trusted more than any other doctor at the time. He was also the first to tell me, "Jon, I am no longer here to keep you alive. I'm here to make you look pretty again." He must not have seen any pictures of me previously. Just kidding. "Dr. Dre" had already prepared for my arrival, and as an oral maxillofacial surgeon (OMFS), he was ready to fix me. I tended to touch my wounds quite a bit, trying to feel how my face looked with scars and open wounds surrounding most of the right side. Since I touched that side of my face a lot, which Sam kept yelling at me to stop, it quickly became infected. My bad. My doctor told me in order to remove the infection, he would have to remove this skin around my eye socket and replace it with a skin flap from another part of my body. I didn't have much to choose from because my once two-hundred-twenty-pound figure now was only one hundred thirty pounds. That's right, ninety pounds gone in a month! Lucky me, they could only get enough skin and muscle from my left thigh.

I was prepped for the first of my many reconstructive facial surgeries. What should have been only an eight-hour surgery turned into sixteen hours under a microscope, with Dr. Dre attaching blood vessels from my left thigh muscle, placing them over my right eye socket. With the surgery being a success, I was taken to the ICU again for recovery. Much to Samantha's surprise, when she saw me, she said it was the most traumatic thing she had ever seen, much worse than what she had walked into when she arrived in Germany. I had a huge piece of skin and muscle where my eye used to be, and since I had been in surgery for so long, they kept my breathing tube in. I did not like that and was choking on it, as well as chewing on it to somehow get it out of my throat. I was also trying desperately to get that tube out, so some of the staff had tied me to my bed with restraints to keep me from pulling it out. Samantha said that what she walked into was like a nightmare or a scene from a horror movie, adding if she hadn't walked out of my room, she would have done what was expected of her in Germany: faint. She and my dad both said they just wanted the next three days to pass. They insisted that the doctors give me medication to sleep, instead of watching me suffer on that breathing tube. Thankfully, the doctors agreed.

I ended up falling asleep. While I slept, I dreamt that my head was in a vise. Someone was cranking down on the vise, and I felt as if my head was about to explode. Knowing that my dad was in the room, I pleaded that he stop the person from cranking down on the vise. My dad grabbed my left shoulder and told me to wake up, saying that no one was cranking down on a vise. Pulling myself out of sleep, I felt exactly what was going on.

Since the flap had produced fluid, Dr. Dre had also added drain tubes, but since the fluid also clotted, he and his staff would have to press down on the skin flap to drain the site. I recall the next morning vividly. Dr. Dre had gauze balled up and was rolling it down the newly installed flap, pushing out the buildup of fluid. This was painful. My reaction was immediate as my hands shot up, grasping his wrist and arm just below the elbow. I was in the perfect posture to position myself for a triangle choke, but since he was my primary doctor, I only held him firm. I believe I dreamt of shifting and putting him in the choke hold, but I didn't do it. Seconds after I had grasped him, he called out to my father for help: "Mike, I cannot move." I smiled, knowing that even after everything I had been through, I still had a fraction of my strength left. My dad wrestled my hands to my side. I groaned as Dr. Dre finished pushing the fluid out as gently as he could, the whole time reassuring me that he was there not to keep me alive, but to make me pretty again.

This event had a few second- and third-order effects. First, from that point on, Dr. Dre made sure I was restrained when he worked on me. Second, Behavioral Health remarked that I displayed heightened levels of agitation. Finally, I knew that I had one of the best doctors working on me, and I was very appreciative of how responsive he was to my needs and requests.

Five months after the explosion and four months after my flap surgery, I would get the pleasure of having another surgery done by Dr. Dre. In addition to my eye injury, there was a wound on the right side of my head that refused to heal. Because my skull was exposed, it needed to be covered as quickly as possible so this area wouldn't get infected again. I was getting ready to be discharged soon to start blind rehab and needed to have my wounds healed beforehand. My recovery at Walter Reed up to this point was happening very quickly, and I was ready to start the next phase of healing. Dr. Dre had a plan to cover the wound on my head with a graft. This was going to be one of the better surgeries, or at least this is what I was told, because the recovery would be extremely fast and painless given the fact that I had no feeling in that spot of my head.

Sitting in the waiting room, I talked with Samantha about a gala we were invited to attend the next day. This would be the first time I would be able to escape the hospital, and I was excited to take my wife out. "What time do we need to leave for the ball tomorrow?" I asked her.

She replied, "I don't know. We will have to wait and see if you can even go. After all, you are having surgery." I told her that I would be able to attend the ball. I was especially wanting to go since it meant dressing up and putting my uniform back on. And I would not miss the chance of being by her side when she got to wear a ball gown. I had already decided that she was going to be the Belle of the ball, which made me the Beast.

"Jonathan Turnbull," a nurse called. I stood up, grasping the back of Samantha's arm for her to lead me into the operating room. Dr. Dre was there. He took control of the situation, telling Sam that he would come get her following the surgery. She gave me a quick kiss and wished me good luck before leaving me at the mercy of OMFS.

Dr. Dre explained that he was going to pull a skin graft from my left leg for the site on my head, right next to the spot where he had taken part of my thigh muscle. I laughed, telling him that the donor site for the skin flap over my right eye that he had taken had finally healed, and now he was taking a skin graft from it. "What did my left leg ever do to you?" I asked.

He chuckled at my inquiry, responding, "You know that I like to have you restrained if possible. Would this be okay as I examine your donor site?

After I'd nodded my approval, I felt his assistant grab my arms and hold them fast to my sides. With that Dr. Dre grabbed my sweats and pulled them swiftly to my ankles. I was surprised to the point that I couldn't even remark on what had just happened, except to say that I was glad I had worn underwear today. Dr. Dre examined my left leg. After seeing what he needed to see, the team escorted me to a surgery chair. They lifted my legs into stirrups commonly used by ob-gyn departments and secured my hands above my head, also securing my legs to the stirrups. I was now able to comment, "Wow, first you drop my pants, then you restrain me to a chair. Most people pay good money for this kind of treatment, and I get it for free. What is my safe word?"

I thought it would bring at least a chuckle, but instead the assistant said, "I am going to administer the fentanyl through your PICC line now." I nodded again, knowing that I was about to be unable to remember anything. After the drug, I asked Dr. Dre, "Can you shave the donor site before the surgery, so I don't have leg hair on my head like the flap?" He turned on the clippers. The only problem was that they were not hair clippers but skin clippers. He started taking the skin graft from my knee and moved toward my groin. I felt everything. After a few moments, I asked him to stop. He waited a few moments for the drug to kick in and then continued. No matter how much fentanyl I'd been given, I still felt the skin removal from my thigh, but he was swift. Before I reached the point where I could no longer stand it, the thing was completed.

Since the doctor couldn't stitch the graft to the skin around it, he had to attach it with a bolster. Being a very adaptive individual, Dr. Dre made his own bolster from gauze and a glove, stitching that to my scalp to hold the graft in place until it took hold. Finally, the surgery was completed with a clear plastic sheet taped to my leg as a giant Band-Aid. I was then I was wheeled out to the waiting room. Sam asked how it had gone, and I angrily stated that I just wanted a Wendy's cheeseburger to go. Early the next morning, while at another doctor's appointment, I described how painful the surgery was. Much to everyone's surprise, my PICC line was clogged and the fentanyl was still in my line. My doctor decided it was best just to take that line out and do IVs instead.

I was given the clear to attend the Luke's Wings Charity Ball with my wife that next evening. We were also going with Heidi, my teammate Devin, and a few other wounded soldiers who were at Walter Reed. Being able to go to this event was an incredible mood booster, providing me with the motivation to get out of the hospital. It was an honor being able to meet with many of the participants and spending time with my friends and wife outside the hospital.

The surgery did not affect me until late in the evening when we were getting ready to leave. My head felt just fine, but my leg was burning and had started to become very irritating. We had decided before the gala to cover my leg with a nonstick gauze pad. That way my uniform pants wouldn't become ruined.

I was staying the night at the apartment where my wife was living. Before going to bed, we decided to remove the bandage to let my wound breathe and apply healing ointment. Much to our surprise, we quickly found the nonstick gauze was stuck. Samantha was blessed with the opportunity to inflict pain on me. She tried her hardest to be as gentle as possible removing the gauze. I never in my life have hit a woman, but this time I had to lie on my arms to prevent from swinging at her. As I previously mentioned, my wife was the Belle of the ball that evening, and I quickly portrayed my role as the Beast, yelling "That hurts!" just like in the scene after the beast fights off wolves and Belle is there to clean his wounds. This pain ranked right up there with when Dr. Dre pushed on my flap. Between him and Samantha, I learned that one must hurt in order to heal.

A few weeks later, I waited for my name to be called in the waiting room of OMFS. After the nurse checked my vital signs, I waited for Dr. Dre, who excitedly told me how good the skin graft looked once he had taken off the bolster. He stated that he thought it best to disinfect the site, if that was okay with me, to which I nodded in agreement. He grabbed a bottle of sanitary disinfectant, poured some into gauze, and started wiping down my graft. Finishing the graft, he moved to the flap and my face. I made fun of him, thanking him for the facial and then the hair treatment. As he was washing my hair, I tasted the liquid by accident. It not only smelled minty but also tasted very minty. Knowing that Dr. Dre was a dentist, I asked him if he was using mouthwash as his disinfectant. He said that he was, which made Samantha and me laugh. Well, now I have had another completely new experience at the hands of OMFS at Walter Reed.

To continue my train of thought about OMFS, Dr. Dre wrote up a note for Samantha to get a handicapped parking sticker since he had cut out a part of a large muscle from my leg and put it on my face. We went to the Maryland Department of Transportation and turned in the appropriate paperwork. After waiting for what seemed an hour, we were informed that the state of Maryland does not recognize dentists as official doctors, even one who completed a sixteen-hour surgery on my face, so they would not give us the sticker unless we got another doctor's signature. We made sure Dr. Dre heard this every time we saw him, but we ended up getting our primary care manager to sign it for us.

It was embarrassing. After we finally got the handicapped parking sticker, we decided to use it at our apartment. Of course, the first time we used it to park, we went to get into the elevator, but it was broken, forcing us to climb the twelve flights of stairs. I was gripping my Taco Bell bag while walking up those stairs, yelling, "Come on, left leg! Work with me here!" I count that as irony. All this aside, Dr. Dre, you are an incredible human, as well as a fantastic surgeon and someone I now consider a great friend. Thank you for making me pretty again, and thank you for the laughs.

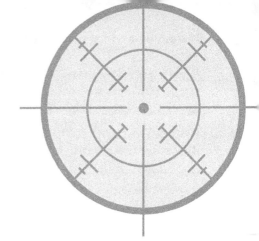

34

Angels, Bagels, and Doughnuts, Oh My!

Man shall not live on bread alone.

—Matthew 4:4

It was a dark night, and I was in a similar mood as on the night when Hadassah appeared to me in my hospital room at Walter Reed. In the depths of my despair, I cried out to God for help and was excited to see how he was going to work in my life. I knew that he was going to do something amazing, such as send one of his angels like Hadassah or Samantha's grandma Doris, or one among several other possible candidates, to my room to help me fight the great adversary. Before recounting this night, I want to thank those whom God worked through, those who worked behind the scenes.

I was placed on a liquid diet, so at any time I could make a request. I asked for special treats. I am partial to doughnuts, which is a commonly known fact to those closest to me. An angel from my hometown decided to show her love by sending me five dozen doughnuts from a place called Cops and Doughnuts. I was an instant celebrity. Thank you, Marcy. Semper fi. I was back to lying in my hospital bed, wallowing in my despair. It was darker than usual, which I marveled at since I couldn't see anyway. Suddenly there was a sound that didn't surprise me since I was deep in prayer for help. There were three knocks on the door, followed by "Captain Turnbull, it is Nurse Gabby. May I enter your room?" Gabby was one of my one-on-one nurses and one of my favorite people. She took great care of me and was very attentive to my needs. I motioned to her to enter, and then I heard something that got me to thinking. "Sir, I saw you were awake. I was eating one of your doughnuts. I have an extra one. Would you like the extra one?" That question lifted my spirits higher than anything else I could think of. A doughnut brought just for me!

"Yes, ma'am. That would be delightful," I responded with a huge smile on my face.

With a delicious sugary treat in my mouth, I tried to produce intelligent and understandable words. "Gabby, may I ask what Gabby is short for?"

She responded quickly with food in her mouth as well. We must not have had any manners in my room. "Gabriella. Why?" she said, lifting an eyebrow to add to her question.

Now I knew the answer before I had even asked my question. "Are you an angel?" She chuckled at that, calling me sweet, and left my room. Without the food, she showed up in my time of need and helped me overcome something that couldn't have been overcome by medicine. Secondly, she had brought me my favorite food on the planet, so there was that. Finally, her name is the same of that of the archangel who oversees angel armies and is a defender of the righteous. Closing my eyes to go to sleep, I knew that God had my back and that I was safe with angels constantly surrounding me.

I like the doughnut story because it is about doughnuts, and they are my favorite. However, before the doughnuts, there was something more awesome. One morning while I was sitting in my room, an infectious disease doctor entered. He introduced himself as Doc Paul and began to ask me questions. That is a dangerous thing to do with a civil affairs guy because we will never stop talking. Upon learning that I was in the Ninety-Sixth Civil Affairs Battalion, the doctor's demeanor changed. "What?! I was in the Ninety-Sixth back before it was split apart," he said. He then proceeded to name people who had been there while he was the surgeon. Most of the names I recognized. We instantly developed a bond, laughing and telling stories about each person. After a couple of hours of chatting, he clapped me on the shoulder and asked me a question that I had been asked often but that was a question no one ever meant: "Is there anything I can do for you?"

I responded with what first came to mind: "Sir, I could really go for a bagel with lox and cream cheese right now. This liquid food diet is a killer. I need some real food."

He nodded and, laughing, said, "You got it, man," as he turned to leave my room. I thanked him for swinging by my room and lifting my spirits just by talking and wished him well. The next morning, he was back in my room with bags and bags of bagels, cream cheese, and lox. He not only had purchased them, but also put some together for me. He handed me a delicious treat, cut into bite-sized pieces. "Jon, if anyone questions where these came from, tell them OMFS." He laughed deep from his stomach. "No one will question that. But seriously, if anyone says anything, have them call my office. I have your back. Anything for an original." An "original" is what we call someone from the Ninety-Sixth. Those bagels tasted very good. Speech Pathology was a little upset that I was eating regular food, but seeing that I hadn't choked on it and died, they let me know they would allow it. From that point on, I ate regular food again. Knowing I could eat regular food I made me request doughnuts quite often.

Doc Paul, thank you for what you have done for me. You have been a part of Team Turnbull from the beginning, and at the point of writing this, you are the only remaining doctor still on Team Turnbull. I am very appreciative for what you have done and continue to do for me.

Samantha and I had the opportunity to make lifelong friendships. We went through a period where we were introduced to some VIPs who had come to Walter Reed and helped bring joy to many patients who were in different stages of recovery. Each visit showed us patients that there were people who cared and that our sacrifices were not in vain.

At the end of March, my dad was with us. He was excited this day, but he wouldn't tell me the reason. All I knew was that he had just spoken with a representative from the USO. I was a little drowsy from my medicine. There was a knock on the door, and a gentleman asked permission to enter my room. Dad shouted out, "Yes, please come in," before I could respond. The individual walked over to my bed and asked about me. After I'd given him a short summary of what happened and who I was, he introduced himself.

"I came to Walter Reed with my son." The man continued walking closer to my bed. "My son is standing next to you and wants to shake your hand." I reached out with my hand, and a very large pair of hands grasped my own in a firm handshake.

"Captain Turnbull, I am Rob Gronkowski." He said it as if I would know who he was, but the name had slipped my memory.

My dad came to my rescue. "Son, he is a famous football player for the Patriots."

"It is a pleasure to meet you, sir," I said while still shaking his hand. The 6'6" man spoke with us for about ten minutes and gave us each a signed jersey. He laughed at me when I said that the team I cheer for is the Detroit Lions and then asked if he would consider coming out of his one-week retirement to play for them. Before he left, my father asked Rob and his father if they would mind saying a prayer for me. Rob and his dad joined us as my dad did the honors and prayed for my healing and a speedy recovery. Rob's dad choked back tears while doing so. It made me happy to know he cared enough to be there.

They left, and Samantha went down to go pick up a snack for me. In the few minutes she was gone, I had another visitor. Much to my surprise, it was another famous football legend and actor. Feeling that it must have been a day for people to visit us, I welcomed Terry Bradshaw gladly. He spoke about who he was in a large, booming, joyful voice. We talked for a little bit about nothing much, and then I heard Samantha return to my room.

"Um, sir, I did not recognize you with your clothes on!" she exclaimed to the visitor. She sounded extremely happy. I thought it was a strange thing to say. She continued, "I'm thinking of the movie *Failure to Launch*, where you had your naked room of course." She giggled as he said that he hadn't heard that one, and then gave her a big hug. Samantha is a huge Matthew McConaughey fan. Since both Bradshaw and McConaughey had starred in the same movie, *Failure to Launch*, McConaughey talked about Bradshaw for quite a while. Sam has always joked that I look just like Matthew McConaughey. Terry agreed.

As we laughed and made fun of each other, we laughed even harder when Terry said, "Samantha, you shouldn't have a celebrity crush on old Matty boy. You need to chase after a much younger man like Bradley Cooper!" I don't believe he convinced her at all.

"Mr. Terry Bradshaw, it was a pleasure to meet you. We are having a very interesting day today. We just met Gronk, who retired a few days ago, and now we are meeting with you."

Terry Bradshaw picked up where my dad had left off: "You know that I was the original TB quarterback and not that other guy?" Everyone laughed. We continued our conversation. It was awesome meeting with Terry. When he left, we had sore jaws from the jokes and roasting. After meeting with us, he left to talk with other patients. Samantha, my dad, and my mother went out in the hallway, but Sam rushed into my hospital room, following Heidi. Heidi was the first to my bed. She told me it was time to get up. "Jon, there is an event happening right now at the USO down the road. I recommend that you go to it with your wife and family. This event will make your entire family very happy, and you can get lunch while down there."

She got my attention with the food, but it was her pitch that it would make my family happy that caused me to make the decision to go. I got out of bed and put my clothes on while my nurse unplugged the machines that were hooked up to me. When I was detached, I walked into the bathroom, counting the steps very quickly as I had learned. After finishing using the bathroom, I grabbed my father's shoulders, and he led me down the hallway to a waiting wheelchair.

My dad had the honor of pushing my wheelchair through the hospital and then down the road to the USO. I know that he struggled because he lost control of the chair while going down a ramp. To my horror, I ran over Ian's foot before Dad caught the chair.

We entered the USO and signed in. My family found a table and positioned me in a spot that had been cleared for the chair. Shortly after coming to a rest, I heard Samantha exclaim, "Oh my!"

I heard voices and recognized my family talking to someone, but I couldn't identify the voice. It was a man's voice with a slight British accent. Sam walked over to my side and introduced me. "Jon, I want to introduce you to Chef Robert Irvine."

I had not been living under a rock, so I knew exactly who this was. Sam doesn't watch television often, but when she does, she has the Food Network channel on. Chef Robert extended his hand, which I found while trying to stand up. He told me to stay sitting down and then sat to my right at the table.

"Tell me what happened to you," Chef Irvine asked. I gave him a watered-down version of the story, then the announcement came that lunch was ready. Chef Irvine laughed and told me a secret. "Jon, they invited me here, and I have to tell you something. I am an amazing chef, so I came here thinking that I would be cooking. I didn't cook any of this, but I want to get you some of it. Are you hungry?" I nodded my consent and thanked him as he walked away. After I'd eaten the plate of food that he had given me, he laughed while commenting, "I could have made this a lot better. These were gross hot dogs and sticky macaroni and cheese. I don't know about you, but I'm a wet noodle kind of guy." I agreed with him.

Chef Irvine and I talked for about an hour about his military service and about life. I was happy to hear him talking with my wife and parents. When it was time for me to go back to the hospital, he stopped by my chair and handed me a business card. "Jon, this has my personal cell on it. I want to continue following your story through your recovery, so tell your wife to call me anytime. And if there is anything I can help you out with, you tell me. Also, tell her that if she doesn't call me, then I will beat her up." It was a nice gesture, and he was not joking. Over the next couple of years, we would meet him again. He has started calling my wife his BFF. There were a couple times when Samantha texted him and he responded almost immediately. I cannot say enough good things about him and the amazing things he does for people. He is an inspiration to me. I knew that he was a good guy and was very thankful that Heidi had made sure that we got to meet him.

As mentioned previously, music plays an important role in my life. In June of 2019, I was invited to my hometown as a guest motivational speaker at a Christian concert event called Big Ticket. Samantha and I agreed to speak in front of the crowd of a few thousand people because Mr. Danny Gokey was singing and Samantha loves his music. Mr. Gokey sang a song that had played on her Pandora radio in North Caroline the day before I was blown up. While Samantha was Bible-journaling at home, while Ian was at school, she had to fight to stay in control of her emotions. Danny Gokey's song "You Haven't Seen It Yet" came on the radio. She is a huge fan of his and had met him in Flint, Michigan, during my deployment two years earlier. During that instance, he did a shout-out video for her, praying that I would stay safe. However, she had never heard this song before then, so she decided to listen to it again on YouTube. The song was released on January 11. Little did she know that it would be her go-to song for the troubling days she would face. While she was in Germany, she listened to it every morning after doing her devotions.

We arrived at the concert an hour early and met with a friend who was given the task of showing us around. The heat was out in force as we walked around the tents and walked up to the stage. Standing behind the stage, I was asked to speak about the miracles God had done for me. Samantha guided me onto the stage.

The stage people were gracious, giving me a chair to sit in while I spoke. I was afraid that I would walk off the stage and roam as I gave my testimony. I got comfortable in the chair and lifted the microphone up to my mouth. "Hello. I am Captain Jonathan Turnbull. On January 16, 2019, I was blown up." I spoke for about fifteen minutes before Samantha whispered in my ear that our time was over and I had to wrap things up. I thanked everyone for listening to my story and for the many prayers.

I felt sad that my time was over, but then a female voice called from behind me, "Jon, Mr. Danny Gokey is here, if you want to introduce him to everyone."

My heart rate increased, knowing that Sam was going to meet her favorite singer. I turned to the crowd. "It is my pleasure to introduce Mr. Danny Gokey." I pulled a Purple Heart challenge coin I had been given at the hospital from my pocket and turned to face the singer. I put the microphone back up to my lips and informed the crowd, "Many officers have coins that they give people in thanks of a job well done. I am giving you my Purple Heart challenge coin because of the inspiration you gave my family in a time of need." I shook his hand and transferred control of the coin over to him by turning his hand over and placing the coin from my hand into his palm.

Sam escorted me off the stage. She and I stood by while Mr. Gokey said hello to the gathered crowd. The crowd made noise when he said that he would not be singing until a little later, then he walked down off the stage and continued to talk with us.

I told him about Samantha's hearing his music on the radio and how it impacted her life. Then I told him about how Christian music had helped lower my ICP in Germany. "Was it my music that helped you?" Danny Gokey asked.

I shook my head. "No, sir. It was Casting Crowns."

He nodded his head and replied, "That is okay. I like them too." After a few hugs and a lot of pictures, we thanked Mr. Gokey for his kindness and for his inspirational music. Samantha ended up going back to his concert that evening with her twin sister and my brother-in-law. I know they thoroughly enjoyed the time they had because Samantha didn't stop talking the whole ride back down to Flint after meeting him. I felt that she was alive, and I liked how music spoke to her soul.

The following day we left my in-laws' house around noon. We had big plans for this day, as was the case for the rest. We went to our friend Terry's daughter's open house and fellowshipped with our family friends for a few hours. We had to leave in the evening because we had been invited to attend a country music concert a few miles down the road.

Earlier in the month, I spoke at the USA BMX race in Nashville. The organizer who invited me had given us tickets to the country music concert that we were heading to now. When Samantha collected our tickets, we found out that they were backstage passes, so we found ourselves in a tent by the stage. Since it was hot out, I sat down in a chair while Samantha and her sister Sarah got drinks.

I felt a slap on my left shoulder, and then a gentleman asked me who I was. I gave him the rundown on who I was, and he asked about what happened in Syria. While I was telling him everything that I could that was unclassified, he interrupted me, saying, "Hang on there one second. I need to grab a drink. Can I grab you anything?" I thanked him but said I was fine.

After he walked away, I turned to Samantha. "Sam, who am I talking to? He acts like we are lifelong friends, but I don't know who it is."

Samantha leaned close to me and spoke softly, "That is Dierks Bentley, Jon!"

I was in shock. I'd gotten to meet a famous singer yesterday, and then today I was meeting a very important singer. I was very familiar with Dierks Bentley, often having played his music in my civil affairs team room while working. I was very excited to talk when he returned. "Mr. Bentley, I want to tell you something about how your music made an impact on my life." Not hearing anything, I accepted his silence as acceptance. "I told you about how I was blown up, but let me tell it in another way. When the bomb went off, I thought of your song 'Black' because my world went black. And then I had to get up, and I felt like a riser, just like you say in your song. Finally, through my whole recovery, my wife has been by my side completing our music with 'Woman, Amen.'" He seemed to be happy hearing that his music had made such an impact on us, but because he was a big star and had other duties to fulfill, he had to start getting ready for the concert. Sam, Sarah, and I shook his hand, said goodbye, and found our seats.

The concert started with an opening band, and then it got better when Dierks Bentley took the stage. He sang a few songs. Then, to my surprise, he said, "I had the honor of meeting an American hero a few minutes ago. He told me about a song that made an impact on him, and he loves the song 'Woman, Amen.' So, Jon, this song is for you." He sang the song. It was an amazing moment to share with Sam by my side. If that weren't enough, we then heard, "Jon Turnbull? Where are you at?" Pointing me out of a crowd, Dierks said a little about my having been wounded. The crowd erupted in applause and gave me a standing ovation. Bentley then sang the song "Riser" and called me out again, saying, "Jon Turnbull, you're a riser." My wife and sister-in-law were in tears, and the crowd of more than ten thousand people, with their cell phone lights out, started chanting, "USA! USA! USA!" It was an incredible moment, one we will never forget. I felt blessed that Dierks Bentley had taken a little time out of his concert to honor me.

Music has always played a role in my life, and now it was an essential part of my recovery. These singers gave me hope for the future by honoring me. It was one of the best weekends of my life, giving me the assurance that I could survive and recover no matter the odds. God bless music and those amazing singers who gave me the time of day.

35

Food and Nurse Jones

Ask and it will be given to you; seek and you will
find; knock and the door will be opened to you.

—Matthew 7:7

In March of 2019 at Walter Reed, after I had finished my daily
activities and appointments, I was settled into my room. Heidi
came up to the floor to visit. "Hey, Jon! You always have something
interesting playing in here, don't you?"

"You'd better believe that he likes his music," Nurse Kara said,
walking into my room. "He likes listening to it on his iPad and gets
us when it stops playing. Having sat in here for a few hours listening
to Lindsey Stirling play her violin, I just about have the soundtrack
to *The Greatest Showman* memorized."

Heidi laughed upon hearing that I listened to music all the time.
She then turned her attention back to me. "Is there anything we can
do for you, Jon?" Heidi always wanted to do something for us, so I
had to think about it. I wanted to do something nice for someone,
and I couldn't think of anyone other than Samantha to do it for.
She had done so much helping me, and our "dating anniversary"

of fifteen years was approaching in the next few weeks. "Heidi," I said. That way she knew who I was talking to. I found it frustrating as a blind man that people would talk at me without addressing me by name first. Many times, I didn't know they were even talking to me, so I would be focused elsewhere, and I hated being rude. "I would like to take Sam out for dinner if the doctors will allow it. Can you put something together for me—without telling Samantha, of course, because I would like to surprise her?"

Heidi was thrilled. She agreed to do something nice for Sam and got right to work. I have always been amazed at how professional the army's noncommissioned officers are. I knew that I could give a request with a little guidance, then sit back and allow the professionals to act unhindered by my big brain. Colonel Jeff told me always to "trust but verify," which meant to give a mission with a little guidance and then trust my subordinates to show me how amazing they are. When I need reassurance, I can verify the plan by asking direct questions and get back a brief from my soldiers. This was a case where I had made a request and was happy with how everything turned out.

Heidi came back to my room a few days later. Since we were alone, she jumped right into our top secret conversation. "Jon, a gentleman named Mr. Steve Lee has asked to help with your surprise. I have everything taken care of. The surprise will be ready tonight around 1700" (5:00 p.m. civilian time). I smiled and was a little confused, but I was also shocked because I mistakenly thought that Heidi had said Stan Lee, the famous comic book writer and creator of Marvel Comics, was helping us. I thanked Heidi for keeping everything a secret from Sam and told her I couldn't wait for the surprise.

Giving someone a little happiness in life is why we exist, I think. I know it makes me happy to make other people happy. I give my everything to you, Samantha, to make it possible. I knew that the road of our marriage had been a rocky one. It was nice to do something to thank Samantha for staying with me through everything I had put her through.

At five o'clock, Heidi came back into my room and let me know that the surprise was waiting in the family room down the hall on my ward. I called Samantha on my room phone and asked her to come to the hospital immediately. She arrived about ten minutes after I had placed the call. After Heidi had told her that I had a surprise for her, Sam and I both followed Heidi down the hallway to the family room. She opened the door and welcomed us to our room for our date. She had overdone it. I couldn't believe what she had remembered from our conversations. First, she had remembered that it was my and Sam's anniversary. Secondly, she had remembered that I was very hungry for a hamburger, so she had two plates set with hamburgers from an amazing restaurant down the road called Woodmont Grill. Third, she had not forgotten a dessert, which this evening consisted of Samantha's two favorites, cupcakes and strawberry shortcake, which Heidi had combined into one by providing strawberry shortcake cupcakes. Last, Heidi had decorated the room with red balloons. She had so many candles lit that the lights didn't even need to be on. To put the icing on the cake, she had songs from Samantha's favorite singer, Josh Groban, playing softly on my tablet in the background.

The anniversary dinner was a great success. I felt Samantha choke up and her tears of happiness fall as she guided me to my seat. We sat down together and shared the best meal either of us had eaten in a very long time. I don't remember much of our conversation from that night, but I do remember that the burger was the best burger I have ever had. It could have been the company, but that burger was delicious.

This simple act of kindness and thoughtfulness from Heidi helped in healing the emotional scars Sam and I had borne. It also brought us back together, closer than we had ever been. Sam and I will be forever grateful to our close friend Heidi and to the Care

Coalition for making this night possible. And thank you, Mr. Steve, for funding the event and aiding in my recovery.

A couple of months later, Heidi told us that Mr. Steve was visiting Walter Reed and wanted to meet us and take us out to dinner. We happily accepted the invitation and requested that we eat at the place where he had gotten the burgers from for our date. Everyone agreed. That is when we saw the power of our host, because we called to reserve a table, and they told us they did not accept any reservations and that if we wanted to get a table, we should just arrive early. Samantha called Mr. Lee and told him we would arrive early to get a table.

We arrived at the restaurant a couple of minutes after leaving the hospital. I felt funny wearing normal clothes, as opposed to wearing my hospital gown everywhere. We asked for a table for six and were told the wait would be over an hour. Sam called Mr. Lee and told him to take his time arriving because of the wait, and a few moments later, the waitress asked if we were the guests of Mr. Lee. Sam looked around, confused, because he had worked his magic and somehow had gotten us a reservation.

We were seated in a corner booth. Our host arrived along with another couple. The second couple was "living" at Walter Reed like Samantha and I were, just down the road in an apartment. We had a lot of great laughs, making fun of our experiences with doctors, nurses, and the DC area. Mr. Steve was gracious in hosting the dinner. To Samantha's surprise, he informed her that his daughter Katie was a chef on the Food Network Channel, once again providing us with a lot more to talk about. The rest of our evening mostly consisted of talking about food, which resulted in our getting overly full by ordering dessert. Much to our surprise, the manager of the restaurant said our dinner was on the house. We left that evening full, happy, and humbled.

A year later, we were honored to be Mr. Lee's guests at the USO benefit gala. He had something else up his sleeve. Being the man of surprises that he is, he told us to meet him downstairs before the event started, saying that friends of his were there whom he wanted us to meet. Before we knew it, we were downstairs hanging out yet again with Rob Gronkowski, Terry Bradshaw, and Robert Irvine. It was a night that we will never forget. Mr. Steve Lee, we can never thank you enough for everything you have done and for the memories that will last a lifetime.

I signed back into the hospital ward. Not long after getting my pajamas back on, I heard a knock on my door. "Captain Turnbull, may I enter your room?"

Pretty sure that it was Nurse Jones's voice, I responded, "Yes, ma'am." I like that everyone thinks that since I lost my eyesight, my hearing is so much better and I have the ability to recognize who everyone is by their voices. Not true. Well, this time I was lucky. It was indeed Nurse Jones, one of the nicest nurses on the fourth ward. She was a no-nonsense nurse who loved her job—and it showed. She checked my vitals from the machine and asked me a few questions to judge how I was doing, especially after having eaten out with my wife and friends.

One question of hers that I answered wrong was, "When was the last time you had a bowel movement?"

I replied with, "I don't know. A few days ago, I think?"

She replied by saying, "Your lower back must be really tight. Can you roll onto your side and let me examine you really quick?" I should have known what was happening since I was an expert in reading people. And given the fact that my wife began laughing hysterically, I should have known to just get up out of the bed and run right out of the room. I rolled onto my side in the fetal position, catching too late the sound of a latex glove snap over Nurse Jones's hand.

"Please tell me that you have tiny fingers," I said to be funny.

She didn't respond in a funny way. "Young man, you about to find out! I need to give you a suppository to get you back on schedule." With that she inserted that horrible capsule. The only thing I could do in that moment was pray and try not to cry. I want to throw up now a year later just remembering the fact.

My wife laughed very hard as I involuntarily thrust my hips forward to the edge of my bed in an attempt to escape life. I may have cried a little. I was the only one not laughing as I lay on my side, hugging my knees and scarred for life, but Nurse Jones told me it was going to be okay. I hadn't felt that bad since SERE school. To cover my shame with humor, I asked, "Now if I fart really hard, can I shoot the suppository across the room?" That did bring a grossed-out chuckle from my wife.

Nurse Jones shook her head, responding, "Maybe, but then I would have to put inn another one." Okay, not doing that then. Long story short, I had a bowel movement very soon after, and I coined the operation Surprise a Tory. I believe that to this day, that phrase is still used at Walter Reed National Military Medical Center.

36

Richmond VA Hospital

The Lord will fight for you; you need only be still.

—Exodus 14:14

I have mentioned before how quickly I healed following the blast. The doctors originally told my wife and parents that I would be at Walter Reed for five years recovering. When I first heard this news at the beginning of March, two months after the blast, I did everything that I could to prove those doctors wrong again. The thought that my son would almost be a teenager by the time I got out was almost too much to bear. I pushed myself as hard as I could and tried my best to get out of my bed as much as possible. I began to receive day passes to show that I could leave the hospital to start rehab.

On April Fool's Day 2019, I escaped the fourth floor. Walter Reed had treated me with nothing but kindness, and I appreciated everyone and everything at the facility; however, true to my heritage, I did not like confinement. No matter how pampered I was with hot baby wipes and warm blankets, I longed for the fresh air and for room to roam. Right before I was about to leave, a doctor came rushing into my room. He introduced himself and said that he was the doctor who had found the bone shrapnel in my right iliac artery. Samantha and my parents couldn't help but cry, knowing that only four short months ago, I had been within seconds of dying, and by some miracle, now I was on my way to start rehab.

Since I am now blind, and since I had improved so quickly, I needed to start figuring out how to live in this shell of a body without being able to see. When I was transferred from Walter Reed National Military Medical Center (WRNMMC) to the Richmond VA hospital, I was very happy to start a new chapter of my life. Knowing there would be many new trials, I looked forward to the ones that awaited me. The intent for my being at Richmond was to begin training as a visually impaired soldier, or so that was what Sam and I had been led to believe. The Richmond VA had a clinic for visually impaired skills orientation rehabilitation (VISOR), but not a clinic for rehabilitation of the blind as we had thought. The focus at Richmond turned out to be my traumatic brain injury, with which the doctors were thorough. I enjoyed the therapy, which consisted of many mind games such as a therapist asking me questions about myself, playing twenty questions or Trivial Pursuit, and reading me a short story and asking me to repeat as much verbatim as I could. This stuff was exactly right up my alley, which is something I never told them. I had trained in this so that I could excel as a civil affairs officer, and I prided myself on my memory.

After a week at the Richmond VA hospital, I grew depressed. What was I doing? Why was I here, and what was the point? How was this helping me recover, and what did I have to do to get away? I knew there was a point, but no one was talking to me, and the staff was less than forthcoming with me. The nights were still the hardest time because Samantha was not allowed to stick around, so I had to stay alone in Fisher House. I worried for her because I could hear gunshots being fired directly outside the VA. I knew it was time to go. I knew she was safe though, and that it was a good thing for her to be out of the hospital, because if she could have stayed, she would have, which not only would have damaged her body, mind, and spirit, but also would not have helped the situation any.

Since I was kept awake with the hustle and bustle of shift change, and because I am a talker who will talk to anyone, I slept very little, which made me grouchy the entire time. I snapped a couple of times when nurses would tell me outlandish things. One nurse, complaining that I had missed an appointment, blamed me for it. She said that since the information was written on the board outside the nurses' station, I had no excuse for having missed the appointment. I didn't even know there was a nurses' station, let alone a ridiculous appointment board, which I couldn't read because I was blind. Another nurse told me that she had written her cell number and the number to the nurses' station on the board in my room in case I needed to reach someone. I had a feeling they were either joking around with me—in which case, good for them—or had no idea who their patients were. While these little things occurred, my frustration grew and grew. I internalized this frustration, and it began to boil, eventually reaching the point of bubbling over. People were commenting to my wife that I was displaying "high levels of agitation."

One night I had had enough. I got up and searched around for a little while to use the bathroom, before finding it for real this time. Once back in my bed, I lay there thinking over my situation. I wanted to use my brand-new cell phone, an iPhone gifted to me from the VISOR clinic, to call my wife for help, but I knew she needed sleep desperately as she also was coming down with a bad head cold. Lying there, I felt that evil presence that I had known many times before. Depression was beginning to sink in on top of my agitation. That evil presence was back, and I knew his power play. Shaking my head no, I was determined not to let him ruin my day, so I started praying and tried to fall asleep. Sleep didn't come no matter how hard I tried, which I was too aware of. This blind thing was extremely hard to get used to. It didn't matter if it was light or dark out; to me it was always dark, and my body couldn't regulate itself to sleep. I caught myself asking Sam, "Is this reality or not?" The harder I tried to sleep, the more frustrated I became, which made me more upset and made my brain start working more and more, making it impossible to fall asleep.

To add to this frustration, I kept hearing the adversary's voice telling me that God must hate me to cast this burden on me and that not only would I never see my wife again, but also I would never be able to see my son again. This depression thing continued to roll downhill, gaining traction and speed like a snowball. Having grown up in Northern Michigan, I knew that a snowball could get huge as it rolls down a hill, so I did everything I could do to stop mine, especially since the bigger it got, the heavier it got. I prayed and prayed for help, and at one point I knew God was going to help. That was around the time when there came a knock on my door and a young woman stepped into my room. She announced herself, as was the custom, and said that she was a chaplain. "I was one floor up praying with a patient and felt God calling me to come down here. If it is okay, I would like to pray with you." I gave her a quick rundown of what I felt was going on. She took my left hand in hers and placed her other on my forehead.

As she prayed for me to have peace, I was thankful for the help. I felt a wave of peace roll over me, and I blessed God for it. The depression instantly left. I felt warm and lighthearted, knowing that everything that had been bothering me didn't matter. The chaplain sat with me for a few moments, just chatting. She listened more than she spoke, taking in my story, which was a relief to me because I didn't feel anyone cared about it enough to hear. She treated me like a human and not just as another patient who needed his bandages changed and pills administered. Before leaving the confines of my room, she said two things that have stuck with me. First, she said, "I will talk with your primary care doctor and make sure he understands your concerns." That made me feel as if I had an advocate. Second, she said, "If you feel like the devil is on your back and you cannot fight him, I want you to think of this metaphor.

You are a soldier, so I assume you like WWE wrestling? Rather than fighting evil in the ring alone, back yourself up to the rope, reach out your hand, and tag your partner in. Jesus will come in with a wild haymaker and will clobber the adversary, giving you a break. You are never alone in the fight. I will always be praying for you, as will my church and, I am sure, hundreds of others. Stay strong and keep the faith." With that she squeezed my hand and said another prayer before stepping out of my room.

So, life is like a wrestling match, and when I feel that I am losing everything, I need to tag in the Creator, who will fight for me? What a great relief to know. God is good. I don't remember anything else from that night because I fell asleep instantly.

The next morning when Samantha showed up to my room, I had to let her know about the incredible spiritual event that had occurred in the night. She was as excited to hear about how wondrous our God is and asked the nurses' station to contact the hospital chaplain and ask him to come to my room. Chaplain Bradley arrived a few moments later, and asked us, "What can I do for you good people?"

I ran through the events of the night and asked what the chaplain's name was. My jaw dropped open at his response, but I shouldn't have been surprised after everything I had been through. He said, "Well, I think I should tell you that I don't have any female chaplains working here at the moment. I think that you had a real spiritual experience."

Lying back on my bed, I could only take a deep breath and think in my head, *Thank you, God, for sending another of your angels to help me in my time of need.* I am nobody significant, I don't have anything special, and I am no more holy than the next person, but God had graced me yet again with his presence, and for that I am thankful!

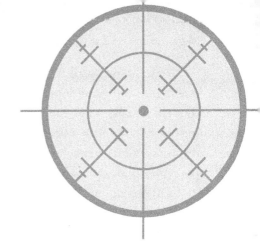

37

Chief's Interment

When you go through deep waters, I will be with you.

—Isaiah 43:2

My escape from the Richmond VA hospital came at the perfect moment. Since I had been unconscious at the time of Scotty's, Shannon's, and Ghadir's funerals, I missed being there for the families of my teammates, something I will regret the rest of my life, even though I couldn't do anything about any of it. I called Heidi and told her that I didn't understand why I was here in Richmond as I wasn't doing anything that involved blind rehab. She was as frustrated as I was and decided to drive down from WRNMMC. We held a group meeting with the doctors involved in my care. I asked if any of them had any reasons why I should remain at the hospital and said that if they didn't, I would be leaving following the meeting. There were a few good arguments as to why I should continue staying there. For example, the doctor in charge of my care boldly said, "Look at your face. You had your whole orbital socket go into your brain. You have a traumatic brain injury, and we want to determine the level of neurocognitive TBI impact."

Nodding my head, I responded, "Thank you for the care and everything you have done for me. I have passed every single test though. And honestly, the reason I am trying to escape your grasp today isn't anything other than the fact that my subordinate and teammate Chief Jon, who was killed in the explosion beside me in January, will be buried at Arlington tomorrow. There isn't anything that will prevent me from being there. If I must, I will do a vanishing act, but I beg you to release me to honor my fallen teammate and be there to support my teammate's widow. Find your humanity, please!"

That was the best I could muster from my Advanced Negotiations Tactics classes, and bless God that it worked. I was discharged from Richmond. Samantha and I drove back to the DC area. It was a memorable drive because it also marked the beginning of my complications from TBI. I would suffer from migraines, nausea, and vomiting with a change in the weather. An hour after leaving Richmond, I was checked into the ER at WRNMMC and had another MRI, which was a routine that would become common for me. The next day, a very sick Jon (that is, me) was still able to stand on his own two feet, which meant I could attend the interment. I wore my military dress uniform, which Chief Mike had brought up for me, as well as my shiny jump boots.

Walking into the family waiting room at Arlington, I didn't know what to expect and was scared out of my mind. The commander of First Special Forces Command was present. He shook my hand before a young woman approached me. "Excuse me. I am Tabitha. Did you know my husband?" I didn't even attempt to choke back my tears. I reached out for her and embraced my new sister. Tabitha, Samantha, and I spoke at great length, and for a moment we felt as if we were the only ones in the room full of people. I found her to be a strong, resilient, and amazing woman. I told her that Jon was in heaven at that very moment, looking down at us, and relayed my conversation with him about death. I cried the whole time, and she kept telling me to be strong.

I commented, "Why am I more emotional than Jon's wife?" She

asked if I would give the eulogy. I said, "If I do, everyone will assume I am gay because I loved Jon so much. He was such a fantastic gentleman. Thank you for sharing him with me." Before long we walked out to the burial site. I had finally pulled myself together. The fresh air, the sunshine, and Tabitha's strength were helping get me through everything.

Sam helped me know what was going on at the interment. Then, just as I heard the single bugle playing "Taps" and General Deedrick began handing the flag that had covered my soldier's casket to his family, I lost it. My emotions got the best of me. I was thinking about not only Tabitha, but also each of the families who had been hurt by what happened to us on the team. I was not only sad but also frustrated that this was even our reality. I turned on my heel and told Samantha I was done and that we needed to get to the car. My knees were not going to hold me up. That was when I heard Chief Mike come up alongside me. "I've got you, brother." He slid an arm around me and said he would help me.

That was when the most amazing moment in my life thus far occurred. As we were walking to the car, I heard a familiar voice asking, "Captain Turnbull, where are you going?"

I stopped, knowing the voice of the most respected man in the entire US military. "That's Colonel Jeff!" Sure enough, it was the same Colonel Jeff from West Point, who was also our boss from Iraq who had appointed me as the team leader of one of his special teams. He embraced me, swatting Chief Mike's shoulder. "Sir," I said, "what are you doing here? Don't you have a war to fight and a team to avenge?" He practically lifted me off the ground. His many Sunday Fun Day workouts were paying off, apparently.

"Jon, I am here for you! I know that you are an emotional kind of guy, so I wanted to be here for you." That is a leader. My own boss was not there, and he lived less than four hours away, whereas my deployed boss, who currently lived in Iraq, had flown halfway around the world to support me today. That is the kind of person I want to be when I grow up. Acting like Billy Maze, he told me, "But wait, there is more." Once he had turned me around, I was almost tackled by yet another person. *What is going on?* To me, this second person was of equal stature to Colonel Jeff.

"Jon, I came here today to be a bedrock for you to lean on too! Why is Samantha still with you?! Now that is an amazing woman." I tried to associate the voice with a face but couldn't quite recall where I last had heard that familiar voice.

Samantha came to the rescue. "Jonathan, how awesome is it that Major Neil is here today?" Lightbulb. *That's right.* That voice belonged to my tactical officer from my freshman year at West Point.

As I have mentioned before, I believe that leadership involves doing for others something that is unexpected but that lifts others up. It is being there in people's time of need no matter the cost. Let me tell you a short story about my history. In 2005, I accepted a nomination to the United States Military Academy at West Point, New York. Go, Army, beat Navy! As a plebe, a.k.a. freshman, I was overseen by Major Neil. He is a colonel now, but he will always be known as Major Neil to my wife and me. This man was one of the most notable officers at West Point, right next to Colonel Jeff, my current boss. Funny how things worked out because they just so happened to be best friends. Major Neil knew everything about me, including that I had a super-hot girlfriend and fiancée at the time, Samantha. He even caught me one day running away from the barracks toward a place called the Round Pond Campgrounds to visit with my fiancée, and he wrote me up for it. During my time at West Point, I don't think I met a more influential individual than Major Neil. I remember going for a run one day and had a nice woman run past me. Knowing that I was a twenty-something young stud who could run like the wind, I was curious who the young woman was, so I picked up my heels and caught up to this mysterious woman. Much to my surprise, when I caught her, she had a huge stomach and informed me that she was pregnant and due very shortly. Not surprising, though, was the news that she was Mrs. Anna, Major Neil's wife. Not only did the man himself display excellence, but also those around him, such as his wife, were examples of excellence.

When Major Neil released me, I heard him walk back to Samantha. After he had kissed her on the cheek and given her a hug, he asked her, "Has Jon grown up yet?"

Samantha's reply was a quick "Nope!" Neil, having assumed as much, told her how happy he was that we were still a couple after so much time. Over the next couple of months, we started attending church with Neil, Anna, and their kids, and Neil and Anna ended up being beside me through the last remaining surgeries I had at Walter Reed. We were able to spend Thanksgiving with them and also celebrate a few other important life events together. I cannot imagine my life without them in it.

God, you have punished me, passing me through the fire. Now having pulled me out of the fire, you harden me and sharpen me into a tool for future use, presenting me with heroes from my past and demonstrating to me perfect leadership and manliness. Thank you for helping me survive to get to this moment that I can now pass into memory. With Tabitha, her children, Chief Mike, Cece, Neil, Jeff, Heidi, my dad, Samantha, and all the others present, what should have been the worst day of my life turned out to be one of the best days of my life. I knew without a doubt that Chief had had a say in all this. He lived to make others happy. *Thank you, God, and thank you, Chief!*

38

Baby Jon

Whoever humbles himself like this child is the greatest
in the kingdom of heaven. And whoever receives one
child such as this in my name receives me.

—Matthew 18:4–5

At Chief's interment, I met a man named Devin. Devin had
come to my hospital room as soon as I arrived at Walter Reed, to
meet Samantha and me, however, I was too drugged at the time
to remember this. Devin was Chief's best friend and is also the
godfather of his children. Chief's oldest son was named after Devin,
and Devin's wife Stephanie was preparing to give birth to their first
son, who was going to be named Jon after our mutual friend Chief
Jon. Samantha and I were instantly drawn to this couple, not only
because of our mutual friend, but also because they were amazing
people. Shortly after the interment, they began experiencing problems
with the pregnancy and began seeking treatments at WRNMMC.
Since they were our friends, we went up to visit with them. I wanted
to do everything I could to help. After losing Jon and going through

what trauma Sam and I had both suffered, I wanted to make sure that they knew we were there for them as emotional support.

One night while I was asleep in our apartment, I had an odd dream where I was in a place of comfort. Chief walked up to me with Jack from the movie *Hook* by his side. Chief told me that the boy's name was Jon and that he was teaching him to play baseball so he could impress his dad when he met him. I knew the dream for what it was since I could see. Before awaking, I hugged both the boy and Chief.

Upon awaking, I felt Samantha crying in bed next to me. Rolling over, I hugged her, asking what I already in my heart knew. "The baby passed last night, didn't he?" My question brought out more sobbing from Samantha. She asked how I knew, so I told her briefly about my dream. We decided that based upon our experiences with the baby we had lost, it would probably mean a lot to our friends to hear about my dream, so we drove to the hospital and went up to their hospital room. The room was packed with grieving family and friends, but we asked if we could talk with Devin and Stephanie alone. We first relayed our story of our baby girl, hoping that it would ease their sense of loss, and then we talked about the dream. The whole time I held Devin's wife's hand. Afterward I hugged my brother. I prayed that our words of encouragement had helped our friends.

A few weeks later, they had the funeral and interment of little Jon. Everything was ready to go, and Sam and I awoke early so we would be able to get there early to help in any way we could. Much to my shame, the weather had changed drastically in the night, and when I awoke, I had a migraine. Before we left, I was not feeling well. We hadn't made it a mile down the road before I told Sam that we had to go back to the apartment because I needed to take some medicine. As soon as we entered the apartment, I started throwing up in the spare bathroom. Samantha was extremely worried because it looked as if I was throwing up blood. I called Devin instantly, telling him that we needed to go to the ER just to make sure I was okay. I have never been so ashamed and will forever be humiliated by that moment. I live to help my friends and family in their time of need, yet I was so sick that I couldn't stop throwing up. After a couple of CAT scans, an MRI, and plenty of fluids and medication, starting with magnesium and ending with morphine, I was discharged, but at that time, the funeral was completed. I pray that Devin and his wife Stephanie will forgive me for what happened. I will never forgive myself for missing baby Jon's funeral. Going to the ER was no excuse. I should have been there. God bless you guys. I love you both.

39

Blind Rehab

I will lead the blind by ways they have not known,
along unfamiliar paths I will guide them; I will turn
the darkness into light before them and make the
rough places smooth. I will not forsake them.

—Isaiah 42:16

Since becoming blind, I haven't experienced anything that has made a more profoundly positive impact on me and given me hope for the future than blind rehabilitation. Shortly after leaving the Richmond VA and making sure I was healthy enough and that my wounds had healed, I, along with Samantha and Heidi, dug deeply into researching the best blind rehab for me. We made sure we weren't going to be going to another VISOR clinic. After trying to decide where to go, we settled on the one place that made the most sense: Cleveland, Ohio.

Since I was in between hospitals, Ian was still living up in Michigan with Sam's parents. That way he had some consistency and could be homeschooled. He was able to enjoy spending time with his cousins too. More than anything, we didn't want him to have to just sit and wait for me to get out of doctor appointments and therapy sessions. Though he was enjoying life, Sam and I missed our son horribly. The Cleveland blind rehab was located near the VA hospital that was closest to Ian, being only four hours away, so on the weekends Sam and I would be able to spend time with him if we could take the time off. The intent behind blind rehab was to show me that what I used to be able to do with vision, I could still do with careful preparation, planning, a good spotter, and care now that I was visually impaired. There were a few moments from blind rehab, though, that will always stick out in my memory.

First and foremost, we called the individuals at the Cleveland VA blind rehab, and they, above the staff at any other facility, fought to get me there, which felt great because it made me feel wanted. We asked my dad if he would mind driving to the clinic to get a tour of the facility and to make sure it was absolutely what I needed. Ian went with my dad. I believe his dimples and his wittiness were what made the nurses want me to be their next patient. I packed my bags and left Walter Reed in June, then headed up to Ohio. Upon my arrival, the people at the Cleveland VA instantly made me feel at home. They asked where our son was and why he wasn't with us. Sam and I laughed because they had a giant calendar that they had decorated just for Ian, having covered it with SpongeBob stickers, and he wasn't with us to see it. We reassured them that he would be visiting as soon as possible.

I was checked into the rehab clinic, and Sam was escorted down the street to the Fisher House, where she would be staying. She felt that she was getting a VIP treatment because this Fisher House had just been built and she would be the very first guest to stay there. The next day would be the ribbon-cutting ceremony. With news reporters and top city officials scheduled to be there, the staff wanted Sam to be in attendance too. Since blindness was new to both of us, they allowed an exemption and let Samantha to stay there with me and help with some of my classes. Normally, patients are dropped off and families aren't permitted to stay because they are a "distraction to learning." I will forever be thankful that the people at this hospital were so flexible not just for me, but also for my wife. They understood that I needed her there.

Sam came back to the hospital. We spent the rest of the day being given a tour of the rehab and getting all my things unpacked. Later in the evening, Sam went back to the Fisher House, and I quickly fell asleep. Excited about starting rehab, I was somehow able to sleep a full night, which was one of the first full nights of sleep unaided by medicine since I'd arrived in the United States America.

Part of military culture is that not many soldiers, or even many officers, care for officers. I don't know if the reason for this is rebelliousness or what, but in my experience, soldiers take every opportunity to make fun of officers. The first morning at blind rehab was one such occasion. I was the youngest person at blind rehab, with the next youngest being in his late seventies. The other veterans there had served in Vietnam, Korea, and World War II. It was an honor to be among them, and I relished the opportunity to chat with them and hear of their life experiences. After getting my morning medicines, I went to breakfast, joining an old gentleman at a table. Someone brought me a tray of mush. I had a hard time figuring out what it was. The gentleman eating with me introduced himself and made conversation. "Excuse me, are you our new officer?"

"Yes, sir. I am new here. I am a captain," I responded to his inquiry.

He continued, "Welcome to blind rehab. May I ask, what is that on your face?" I was taken aback because I didn't know anyone at blind rehab could see. I sure couldn't. Touching my skin flap that covered my right eye, I said, "This is a skin flap that was put over my eye to heal an infection."

The older gentleman continued, "Interesting. Is it sensitive?"

"Yes, sir it is very sensitive. It was put on a few weeks ago." I continued to play with the gruel in front of me.

Samantha had joined me by this time. She was attracting attention because she was the only woman at blind rehab who wasn't a nurse and was not blind at all. I was struck by something I had not see coming at blind rehab: "Sir, if it is sensitive, did it come from your manhood?" I choked on my breakfast and dropped my utensil on the table. My wife tells everyone that this is one of the first times she had ever seen me speechless, and as far as I can remember, I think she may be right. *Why on earth would he ask this?* I thought. The old man continued, "If it is, we've got some pretty good names we can call you by." He was proud of himself, and I was kind of amazed.

Samantha, coming in for the save, said jokingly, "No, sir, they didn't take it from his manhood. It isn't that big. They took it from his rear end, so there's a whole lot of other names you can call him!"

I still had no words besides "I'll break an old man's hip!"

I would pay that gentleman back that evening.

Samantha was able to spend time with me in my room until 1900, and then she had to return to her room at the Fisher House. I smiled, feeling as if we were dating again. Before she left, we heard a loud noise coming from the hallway. Someone was screaming at someone else. Since I was one of the higher-ranking individuals, I went out to investigate and provide help if I could. As I trailed, keeping my hand on the wall so I wouldn't bump into something or get lost, I walked toward what I figured was a patient yelling at a nurse. The closer I got, the more certain I became about was going on by the nurses' station where we received our nightly medications.

"You will not be giving me a shot. I demand that only pretty nurses give me shots. Where are all the pretty nurses?" a patient was yelling at one of the nurses. At that point I was about five feet away. Realizing that this was the same guy who had made fun of my flap that morning, I interrupted.

"Excuse me. This is Captain Jon. May I be of assistance? Sir, you should probably calm down before your pills become suppositories." I then told the gentleman good luck and returned to my room.

A couple of weeks later, Ian arrived to stay with Sam, and we had an interesting experience with another blind veteran. Our rooms were outfitted with Amazon Alexas, which we would use to listen to music at all times of the day. Ian was a stinker and would go up and down the hallway setting the ancient veterans' alarms to play some hip-hop music. He even got me a couple of times. This night I was lying in my bed while Samantha and Ian were sitting in my chair watching *Wheel of Fortune*, Samantha's favorite TV show. While we were listening to music on the Alexa, a gentleman walked into my room. All the rooms there were the exact same layout, so patients sometimes got confused. I had found myself accidently walking into other rooms too, so I didn't fault this old guy. But it was funny. After he walked in, he went over to the Amazon Alexa and, according to Samantha, leaned over it and yelled, "What is that noise?!"

It surprised me. After a few moments, I spoke up because Samantha was trying her hardest not to laugh. I said, "Sir, I think you are in the wrong room."

Startled, he responded, "I am sorry. I am so embarrassed, but I am glad that you caught me before I got naked and climbed into bed." I was too.

After he left, we laughed.

That Alexa was nice for listening to music, but it did give me a few scares. During therapy one day, I was working on my computer with Paul, my computer-assisted technology (CAT) therapist who was also visually impaired. I counted him as one of my most valuable therapists. He impressed me because he had never in his life seen a computer or cell phone yet was teaching me how to use both! While crushing some computer work, I had my Alexa playing softly in the background. At this time, I had it set to play random music that I liked, but unbeknown to me Ian liked some strange music that was also playing. Samantha came into the room at some point and asked why we were working in the dark. She flicked the lights on and then quickly apologized at the silliness of her question to the two blind guys working in the dark. We laughed at her. Then Paul stopped me working and asked, "Jon, what are you listening to?"

Not knowing I had ordered my Alexa to play volume six, which was a mistake, I became instantly confused and embarrassed. The music playing was supposedly kids' music, but it was nothing I would ever let my son listen to. "I'm a banana! I'm a banana!" is what we heard before I yelled, "Alexa, thumbs *down*!" I laughed and told Paul I had no idea what it was. I would have to make a point to beat up my seven-year-old son sometime in the future for having liked such a weird song on my device. Good job, Son. You got me.

Another evening, I wandered around until I found the nurses' station. A young woman named Chelsea, who always gave me a hard time, helped me to a seat where I would take my nightly medication. I went to take a seat and apparently was about to completely miss it. Seeing this, the nurse reacted instantly, reaching out to stop me. The only thing I felt was her hand tightening on my rear end. Her quick response ended up working great because it made me straighten up quickly and blush a deep red. I am pretty sure I told her, "Get ahold of yourself, ma'am. My wife is right there."

We still laugh about it, especially because of her quick reply: "You are such a handful, Jon!"

Over the next twelve weeks, blind rehab was full of eventful moments, but since I'd been wounded overseas, I finally felt that I had a purpose again. I loved my instructors, and the men and women who were going through struggles similar to mine were a comfort when I needed them most. To know I wasn't alone in this dark world, fighting battles I couldn't talk to anyone else about, was something I needed more than I knew. I am very thankful that the Cleveland VA made many exceptions for me because of my situation and allowed Samantha to stay with me. She sat back and watched others show her how she would be able to help me once we got back home; she learned how to put bump dots on our appliances to make it easy for me to do simple daily activities; and most importantly, she was able to learn how to walk me and lead me. We were able to go sailing, attend baseball games, go to a Home Run Derby, visit the Ohio State School for the Blind (which was very inspirational to us both), go golfing, and most importantly spend a lot of quality time together, something we hadn't ever done since becoming married.

Every week we went fishing with my instructors Shawn, and Jason, and though I barely caught anything, Sam showed off and never left without catching something. I mostly went fishing because beforehand, we always went to a restaurant called Barrio that served the best tacos I'd ever had. I never knew that pineapple belonged on tacos, but once I had it, I couldn't believe I had never tried it before. No matter how good or bad our week was, we always enjoyed the weekly fishing nights, even if it just for the tacos and being able to sit in a lawn chair and listen to the waves of Lake Erie.

Once I got the hang of blind rehab, I started getting daring, which wasn't anything outside the norm for me. I began requesting as much time away from the hospital as I was allowed, and I spent increasingly larger amounts of time with my family. Ian started staying with Samantha at the Fisher House quite a bit, and I found that the bigger of a stinker I was at blind rehab, the more amenable the staff was to let me go, because then they wouldn't have to suffer having me around. One such night when I was free, it was one of our more interesting times together as a family. I requested my first pass to stay at the Fisher House, and thankfully I was given permission to stay Ian and Sam. This was the first weekend alone with just Sam and Ian outside the hospital. I was very excited.

We went to an amazing German restaurant together for dinner, which evoked strong emotions in both Samantha and me, and then we returned to the Fisher House. After the amazing dinner, we spent a fun evening together watching *SpongeBob*, *Wheel of Fortune*, and *Jeopardy!* Very excited about being able to sleep in a normal bed, I crashed early. Around three o'clock in the morning, though, I awoke, feeling unwell. My head was beginning to hurt, which, as we had begun to understand, usually led to a migraine. This would lead to nausea and vomiting if left unchecked, so I took some medication and Sam and I prayed before I attempted to fall back asleep. The medication didn't work as we had hoped. Around five o'clock in the morning, I told Samantha I needed to go to the hospital because there was something wrong. We got dressed quickly and rushed to the blind rehab. Not only had my headache reached a peak pain level of eight out of ten, but also my back had started hurting at a pain level of nine out of ten, which was unusual for me. Samantha asked if it was my kidney because I was acting like a pregnant woman in labor.

We walked into blind rehab. The nurses were confused to see me because I usually didn't show up until breakfast, which was around eight o'clock. We told them that I needed fluids delivered in some other way than orally to help drop my headache, but they were not allowed to give me an IV. I started throwing up right then at the nurses' station. After some discussion, I rushed myself to the emergency room, where I was told they could not treat me because they had no neurology department. They called for an ambulance. The ambulance drove me to the Cleveland Clinic, where I was admitted instantly.

I still had a large hole at my right temple because my skin graft had ended up failing while at the VA, so my head was wrapped. This and my skin flap were the only things the ER doctors and nurses could see, no matter how much I told them that I was in immense back pain. They ordered an MRI for my brain and, fearing a stroke, also ordered an angiograph, which took pictures of my brain from inside my body. I was wheeled down to an operating room and was asked to disrobe. Once I was naked, I lay down on the table. While waiting there, one of the strangest things that has ever happened to me occurred. A nurse walked up to me and without announcing herself or notifying me what she was doing grabbed my manhood and taped it to my stomach. This startled me more than anything had ever startled me before. I demanded that if anything else was going to be done, I be told first because I was blind and couldn't see what was happening.

After I'd had my femoral artery cut and a camera inserted, traveling to my brain, pictures were taken showing that I had blood on my brain but no major stroke. The doctor made sure to apologize for the taping incident. "No matter how bad life will get for you as a blind soldier, you must remember this moment and know that you will never be a genitalia taper."

My mom ended up coming down to Cleveland to spend time with Samantha and me. Ultimately she took Ian home for us. Eventually I was released to go back to the VA. I hadn't had a stroke; however, I had presented as severely dehydrated and—surprise!—pregnant with a kidney stone. Once again, Sam had been right. I told her I thought it was time she went to nursing school. Who am I kidding?! I need her more than I need anyone else. After a week at the Cleveland Clinic, I was ready to be back to the VA to finish up my time there.

I chose to serve in the army having been heavily influenced by my family, who took service to our country seriously. My father worked for the state of Michigan keeping everyone safe from bad people. My aunt and uncle were police officers for the city of Flint. My grandfather retired the year I was born, and the same day returned to work as a homicide detective for the City of Flint, solving cold cases because it was the right thing to do. Growing up, I knew that I wanted to do something that would give me the ability to avenge that which could not be defended and protect people who could not protect themselves. Since I was smart and strong, I chose the military to serve not only my country but also the world.

While I was at blind rehab, my nurses took me, my family, and some of the other patients to a place where a gentleman and his wife had decided to serve the world through creating joy and handing out smiles, but in a very different manner from what one would expect. With Ian visiting, we loaded up on a bus at the Cleveland VA and, as expected in the north, froze for the entire hour bus ride. We were transported to a location called Santa's Hideaway Hallow, which grated on my nerves because it was July; why would we go see Santa in July? I was pleasantly surprised by the place, though, and Ian loved it. We started off the adventure fishing, which is Samantha and Ian's favorite hobby. Ian caught a huge catfish. After fishing and grabbing a bite to eat, it was our turn to explore. We met a Native woman who told us a story about her people from her tepee, then we took Ian to Santa's workshop. While sitting on Santa's lap, Ian presented Santa with his Christmas wish list: "Santa, since you are old, I know you will forget what I want, so I wrote it down," Ian said while presenting Santa with a handwritten note.

Santa put his glasses on and looked over Ian's short list. After reading it over, he put his hand to his forehead, put Ian on the floor back on his feet, and read the letter, as follows: "Dear Santa, this year for Christmas, I would like (1) a drone, (2) one thousand dollars, (3) eyes for my dad to see again, and (4) for ISIS to be eliminated."

Santa got choked up and grabbed my hand. Looking up at me, or so I thought, he asked, "Sir, If I can accomplish number three, can you help me with number four?"

I squeezed his hand and nodded. "Absolutely, Santa. Those terrorists won't know what hit them if I can see again. My battle cry will be, 'For God, country, and Team Manbij!'"

We got a family picture with Mr. Claus, then Mrs. Claus drove us around in Santa's golf cart. Ian got his hair cut by an elf and insisted that Sam get something done to hers. Much to her dismay, Sam got her hair braided with some pink hair coloring in.

When it was time to leave, we loaded on the bus. Much to our surprise, unlike the trip to the Hideaway, the ride home was hot because the air conditioner wasn't working. Once I'd arrived back to the VA, feeling hot and being covered in sweat, one of my favorite instructors, Jess, did something that left me speechless (and not for the first time). Leaning over to our son, Ian, she simply said, "Ian, I'm all swampy, if you know what I mean." We quickly changed her nickname to Princess Fiona, from the movie *Shrek*, and went back to my room, laughing the whole way. Overall, it was a fantastic day, one I will always remember.

I worked my tail off the next few weeks at the VA, and once again I asked for a pass to leave. With an approved pass, I left blind rehab. Sam and I drove north and decided to stay a week at a campground in Howell, Michigan, for the last week of July. I had completed most of my journey at blind rehab and was excited to put into practice everything I had learned up to this point. It was time to see if there had been a point to blind rehab. I had the feeling that I was not going to be disappointed. Very good friends of my family who lived at the campground had invited us to stay with them. I am pretty sure I stayed with them as much as with my own parents growing up. I counted their children as close as brothers and sisters, as close as my own. After arriving at the campground and dishing out long-awaited hugs, Samantha and I walked over to a small church where Ian was attending children's church. He had spent the previous weeks with his grandparents and didn't know that we were going to be at the camp this week, so we wanted to surprise him. Walking into the building, I was overwhelmed by emotion upon hearing the children praising God through song. Having spent many long hours in this building growing up, I felt very blessed that my son was able to experience the overwhelming presence of God as well.

The children's pastor and his wife who were in charge while Samantha and I were children were still running things. They saw that Samantha and I and had a plan. They called Ian to come up in front of the other kids. While praying for him, they asked if he missed his parents. He responded that he did. Then they told him to open his eyes. By this time, Sam and I were standing in front of him. He embraced his mama, and Samantha started crying tears of happiness. It had been a few weeks since we last were with Ian, so this was a joyful moment. After children's church, I drove our family to the big church in a golf cart, with the assistance of my second mom, Kim, telling me to go left of right to stay on the path. Even blind, I knew my way around. Church camp was a very important place for us.

In 2001, while I was working as a lifeguard, I encountered a twelve-year-old girl holding a little black dog named Cole on a leash. Cole was the dog of a friend of my family, so I approached the girl, who I thought was beautiful, and started talking to her, asking how she knew this dog that I also knew. Easy pickup line for a fifteen-year-old. By the end of the week, this girl, whose name I'd learned was Samantha, was one of the most amazing young women in the world. Her grandmother told us that one day we would be married and that we made a great couple. Eighteen years later, our beloved deceased grandmother had proven to be correct in every manner. We loved church camp, and we were excited to be at the place where we had met and fallen in love.

While at the big tabernacle for the adult church, I was honored by the pastor, who asked me to say a few words. God placed on my heart the urge to recount the attack and say a few words about Ghadir, Scotty, Shannon, and Chief regarding their heroism and their sacrifice. The rest of the week we spent with friends of old and lived off campfire s'mores and hot dogs. By the end of the week, I felt that my batteries had been recharged, and I was excited to get back to blind rehab. I learned that just about everything taught at blind rehab was useful, even if I didn't think so. I saw the practical uses of my cane and my OrCam and had discovered that I could do just about everything I had done with vision now, without vision, as long as I had a good spotter. We did a lot of fishing and sat around many campfires, enjoying life. We hadn't had this amount of downtime for what seemed to be forever. I know it will be a week we remember always, and I am very thankful that the VA worked with us to allow this week to happen. I knew I was getting to the point of just wanting to be done. I missed the simplicity of life, just me, my wife, and my son. I missed my bed. I missed sitting on the front porch just soaking in the sunsets. I missed my friends coming over to shoot at our range, and I missed the weekend family cookouts. More than anything, I missed being home.

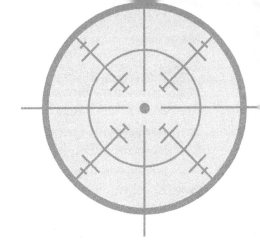

40

"Little Mama" Amina

Many women have done excellently, but you surpass them all.

—Proverbs 31:29

Something I did not think would happen at blind rehab happened, and it ended up being the most amazing thing to happen there: I got a phone call from someone who now means the world to me. This young woman has stolen my heart, and I will forever hold a special place for her there. Just the thought of her warms my soul. I believe I would do just about anything for her. This was an instance of cards falling into place in a strange way.

My phone rang. I was just learning how to answer the silly thing. Still not a fan of iPhones, I had learned earlier that week that a two-finger double tap answers the phone. I was getting good at it. I answered the phone before Siri announced who was calling, so I was not prepared to hear a shriek in my ear: "Yawhaeeeeleeeeeeeeeeeeeee!" This was the battle cry of Ali, one of my linguists, who had worked with Ghadir and me in Syria. At the sound of his voice, I almost dropped my phone. I was silent and didn't know how to speak, which for a civil affairs officer is rare. Ali had called because he wanted to catch up and see how I was doing. We spoke at great length about everything under the sun. Besides Devin, Ali was the first person I'd had contact with since Syria. He told me what had happened following the explosion and how much they missed me. I was very happy to hear his voice.

Choking back the same sort of tears I am crying right now as I type this, I broached a topic he knew was coming: "Ali, I need help. You are good friends with Ghadir's family. I cannot keep going with the status quo. How are they doing? Do you think I could talk with them? Also, do you think it would help heal their wounds if I were to reach out to them?" The silence seemed to last an eternity before he responded. "Jonno, I will send you Amina's cell number. That is Ghadir's mother. She would love to hear from you." My heart skipped a beat. Before Ali hung up, we talked about culturally appropriate things I could discuss with Ghadir's mother to help heal the wounds brought on by Ghadir's passing. It was a moment of healing. It felt amazing to know that I had not been forgotten and that there were still people in the world who cared how I was doing.

That day I received Amina's cell number. With my hands sweaty, I told Siri to call her. The phone rang two times before I heard the voice of an angel. I chuckled, knowing that Amina had sent the call straight to voice mail. I don't answer unknown numbers myself, so I couldn't blame her. Her voice was a replica of Ghadir's. I left a voice mail, then reluctantly double-tapped the phone, hanging it up.

A few weeks later, I escaped another hospital. This time I had to return to WRNMMC to start the final run of surgeries to get myself back on my feet. My time at the VA had ended, and as hard as it was to leave, I was excited to finish up surgeries and get back to a "normal life." As I was sitting in my comfortable chair watching TV in our apartment, Samantha's phone rang. She answered it. After talking a few moments, without saying who was on the phone, she ran to my side and thrust the phone in my hand, telling me to say hello. I put the phone to my ear and had the wind knocked out of me again. Somehow Ghadir's voice was on the other end.

"Jon, this is Amina. I am Ghadir's mother. You called me a few weeks ago, and your wife friended me on Facebook." With tears starting to stream down my face, I sat and listened. "Thank you for reaching out to me. I have been so lonely since my baby was killed, and it was a blessing to hear from you." I couldn't figure out how to speak. When I finally could say something, I asked Samantha to coordinate things so we could travel down to Atlanta to meet with Amina.

Not only did my wife do just that, but also she did it at no expense to us. Samantha amazes me every day. We planned to go to Atlanta as soon as we could. She suggested we contact the Veterans Airlift Command, a volunteer airline company that transports veterans free of charge. What an incredible program! It just so happened that my best friend from West Point and from my Armor Basic Officer Leaders course, who was also a member of the Four Horsemen, had arranged for us to watch the Army–Georgia State football game that same weekend, so we were there for business too.

Landing at Atlanta, Sam and I took an Uber to our hotel, where we quickly checked in. For some reason it was absolutely freezing in Georgia during our time there. Samantha turned the heat on in our hotel room. Much to my surprise, and just our luck, turning the heat on caused the fire alarm in our room to go off. Not only am I blind, but I had now become momentarily deaf.

I was nervous and excited to get to Amina's house. I told Samantha everything I knew about Amina. Ghadir had said that she'd gotten her best attributes from her mother, including her height (she was almost six feet tall), her beauty, her singing ability, her cooking skills (thank God Amina was preparing dinner tonight), and her hookah-creating skills. My heart raced as we pulled up to Amina's house. I got out of the Uber. As I walked up the driveway, I heard the front door open and Samantha say that Amina was at the door waiting for us with tears in her eyes. I braced for whatever was coming and prayed for the best.

After telling us of many hardships, and the few broken hearts that Ghadir had suffered from past boyfriends, I found myself comforting Amina. Hugs are the best way to comfort someone, and I know Ghadir would have wanted me to embrace her mom. As I said, Ghadir stood at about six feet tall; I had anticipated Amina to be similarly tall. After Amina had hugged Sam, she came in for a famous Jon hug. I leaned forward to hug her, my arms outstretched. Upon wrapping my arms around her, I found nothing but hair. Much to my surprise, Amina was maybe five feet tall—my first shock. Ghadir had lied about this one. After I'd patted Amina's head and had figured out the whole height thing, which hug did something that I cannot explain, except to say that my thoughts vanished and I knew that life would continue as it should.

Amina not only sounded just like Ghadir but also acted just like her. Amina grabbed my arm and dragged me into the house, where I met Ghadir's sister and brothers. Amina finished dinner while Samantha and I sat at the dinner table. Then we ate the most delicious food. Dinner consisted of a common dish that Ghadir used to make in Syria, which was lamb kabob, rice, tabbouleh, and flatbread. I definitely tasted in Amina's food that Ghadir had learned to cook from her mom. It was fantastic. I wish I could have eaten more than I did, but I was too excited and was talking too much to eat much of anything. Once Amina had finished eating, I asked her to stand by our end of the table, saying I had something I wanted to do to for her.

Pulling a special something out of my pocket, I stood to face her. "Amina, while deployed, I spent more time with Ghadir than I spent with anyone else. She helped shape and mold me into the person I am today. Even after the evil I beheld, I know there is good in the world because of your daughter. While unpacking my gear and clothing, Samantha found a sweatshirt of Ghadir's that had gotten mixed in with my belongings. She knew it was Ghadir's because in the hooded part of the sweatshirt, she found a few strands of long, dark hair. We searched high and low and found a beautiful locket. If you look inside, you will see it has your daughter's hair in it. Please accept this as a token of my appreciation for the love and kindness your daughter bestowed upon me. I know it isn't much, but it is all we could think to do with it." I handed the locket to Samantha, who gave it to Amina, who told us to forever call her "Little Mama," which of course we will.

I then asked Ghadir's sister and brother to stand, and said, "I am sorry for your loss. You two have to be some of the toughest kids on the planet. I want to thank you for being strong through this trial." I pulled something out of my pocket for each. "I am about to do something that is just for us. This is not official in any capacity, but if anyone challenges it, have them call me and I will do my best to crush them." I lifted a ribbon up. "This is a medal that was minted during World War II, in anticipation of the invasion of Japan. We still use them today. These ones here represent the one I received for the wounds I received on that horrible day when your sister lost her life. This is a military award known as a Purple Heart, and I want you both to have it. I recognize that you both suffer emotional trauma, but you have both endured, have overcome, and have triumphed. I cannot replace that which you have lost, but I want to heal what I can, so in addition to the Purple Heart, let me give you something else." I pulled another medal from my pocket. "This one is the fourth-highest award given to soldiers for valor during combat. For your ability to stand tall through this adversity, I want to give each of you a copy of my Bronze Star. I encourage each of you to always stand tall, especially in the face of your enemies. Last but not least." I was full-out crying by this time. Samantha had to stand behind me with a hand on my back for encouragement. "I don't cry much; I am sorry." Everyone chuckled. I pulled a couple of coins from my pocket. "As the team leader, I minted a memorial coin in honor of my team. These coins are to inspire and provide hope to anyone who holds them. I want to give each of you a coin, including you, Little Mama. I know coins and medals don't replace Ghadir, or anyone else for that matter, but I prayed over these, and I hope they give some form of comfort."

The next thing I knew, we were introducing our Little Mama to her new grandson, Ian. We had left Ian with my mom in

Washington, DC. He had the funniest story to tell us, with laughter being something we greatly needed. While chatting on FaceTime, we heard Ian say, "Mama—and everyone, I guess. Something bad happened. I had to pass gas, but Mama, it wasn't that! I messed my pants. I can't believe it!" He giggled, as did each of us.

"Ian!" Samantha said. I laughed and was very happy to hear Amina laughing as well. That was how we would finish the evening. Rather than finish the night off wallowing in death, we ended up laughing about a six-year-old going to the bathroom in his pants, poor little dude.

Samantha and I ended up staying at Amina's house until almost two in the morning just getting to know Amina. It was awesome, so much so that we decided to go back over after waking up the next day. Amina had asked if it would be all right with us if she took us to Ghadir's burial site the next day before we left to go home.

Arriving the gate, we found that it was locked. Amina made us laugh by telling us the thoughts she had of trying to break into the cemetery. With her being just shy of five feet tall, the thought of throwing her over the gate, and getting myself over too, seemed an impossibility. Thankfully the gates would be opened again in an hour, so we went back to her house. She cooked breakfast as we enjoyed some tea. Once back at the cemetery, I choked back tears as Samantha described how beautiful Ghadir's headstone was: black marble with Ghadir's sunrise, and sunset dates. I placed a rose on her headstone, glad it was raining out; that way, no one could tell the difference between the raindrops and my tears.

Amina needed to go to work, so we said our goodbyes. Sam and I made our way to the airport. I know that God places signs in our lives to remind us we will be all right. While going to get a snack for the flight home, Samantha noted a stand of key chains with names on the fobs, arranged alphabetically. In vertical order were the names Ian, Jon, Ghadir, and Sam. Samantha sent a picture to Amina, adding our thanks for her hospitality and love. It was the perfect ending to the most amazing weekend.

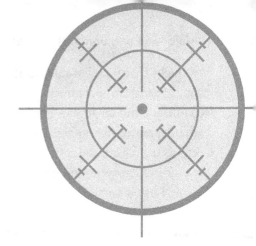

41

Army Ten-Miler

Let us run life's race with passion and determination.
For the path has already been marked out before us.

—Hebrews 12:1

In Syria, I worked out an average of three times a day, doing strength and conditioning workouts twice a day and an endurance / cardio workout once a day. I felt at the top of my game, so after the explosion, having to spend every second in a hospital bed that was not designed for comfort, I was miserable. I loved it each time I had to use the bathroom because it was a chance just to get out of the accursed bed and stretch my legs. I found myself wandering the hallway with my nurse every night around three o'clock. My nurses, Spratley and Gabby, were always there to assist me. It was my favorite part of the day.

I started looking for any opportunity to get out of bed. The PT program was not as nice as I had hoped. They had put me on a new step machine, which I rebelled against almost instantly because I was a runner and wanted the opportunity to run again. Going from my two hundred pounds in Syria to roughly one hundred thirty, I thought that now I would be able to run like the wind, but I was not given the opportunity. I ran a couple of times with Samantha while at blind rehab, but never running farther than a half mile, at the request of my doctors. My former company commander Ryan contacted me around July and told me that he had signed me up for a race in October—and not just any race, but the Army Ten-Miler. Now I had a mission and a goal.

When October arrived, not having done any additional training, I knew I would have to rely on sheer grit, stubbornness, determination, and will to complete the race. I met up with Ryan, and he and I signed in. The following day, we met up at the start line. I had the most amazing support group running with me: my sister; my company commander; my previous TAC officer Neil; Vince and Igor, two friends of mine from when we lived at Fort Stewart; and the wife of Vince, Shannon. Cheering us along the way was Samantha and my dad.

The race was not an easy one. We ran with the Wounded Warriors because of my status, which made it such that we would not be a hindrance to any of the professional athletes. A member of the army's Joint Chiefs of Staff approached me and presented me with his coin before the race to honor me, and then we racers were off. I felt as if we'd been running for hours before asking Ryan, a.k.a. Slaw-Dawg, how far we had gone. He said we were about to finish the first mile. I had known this was going to be a long run, but since my sister had not run more than a few miles her entire life, I was inspired by her and knew I could finish. There were hundreds of people monitoring my race through social media (notably, my goddaughter Rain), so I had plenty of motivation to keep my feet moving.

Along the way, a young woman who tried to run around our pack tripped over a cone and hurt herself. Ryan yelled at me, "Jon! A woman just killed herself." I shook my head, telling him that he should choose his words more wisely because with me being blind, I must take him literally—and I didn't think that someone had just actually killed herself.

By the grace of God alone, we finished the race. I was proud of my teammates. Each person had the names of Team Manbij servicemembers on their running bibs, which really humbled me. I thanked each of them with one of my team's coins.

Since I had not trained for the race, I was hurting badly afterward. The next day I had to hold onto Sam's shoulders just to walk anywhere, remaining hunched over at her height. When I wasn't using Sam to walk around the apartment, I had to crawl because my legs didn't work very well, if at all. Thankfully, my sister was the same way, and so was my hero Major Neil. We were able to joke about it, which I'm grateful for. I was very happy to have been hurting now because so many people had said I inspired them by finishing the race, even my goddaughter Rain, who lives overseas in Jordan. I decided then and there my life goal, namely that at any opportunity, I will say yes to any challenge that comes my way.

I will live my life for my teammates and will overcome every obstacle that appears in my way. Since running the Army Ten-Miler, I have been running as much as I can and working out almost every day with a professional strength coach, and mentor, Jason. I've been rock climbing, golfing, and horseback riding. I'm even getting back on the shooting range. One day I want to do everything I used to be able to do. I know I will be able to. I hope I can encourage everyone to step outside their own comfort zones and try new things. There is so much to do in this world, and so many people miss out on things that they are afraid they cannot do. You don't know what you can or cannot do unless you try it.

You now know of my story and the trials I faced. But my story is yet to be finished. There is always a way to yes. Being inspired by my little friend Noah, whom I met at the Library of Congress, I told him—and I will end by telling you the same thing—"No matter what you face, stand tall and say, 'Challenge accepted.'"

Strength and honor!

"Oppressors Beware. Actions, Not Words."